BEHIND THE SCENES OF TIFFANY GLASSMAKING

BEHIND THE SCENES OF TIFFANY GLASSMAKING

THE NASH NOTEBOOKS

Including

TIFFANY FAVRILE GLASS

by Leslie Hayden Nash

Martin Eidelberg and Nancy A. McClelland

St. Martin's Press

In association with Christie's Fine Arts Auctioneers

NEW YORK

Grateful acknowledgment is made for permission to reproduce the following photographs:

Pages vi and 190–91: Collection of the Louis C. Tiffany Garden Museum, Matsue, Japan. Photo: Christie's Images, New York 2000

Pages xi, 15, 134–35, and 171: Collection of the Louis C. Tiffany Garden Museum, Matsue, Japan. Photo: Christie's Inc.

Book printed and bound in Singapore

Jacket printed in the United States of America

www.stmartins.com

ISBN 0-312-28265-6

First Edition: November 2001

10 9 8 7 6 5 4 3 2 1

CONTENTS

FOREWORD

We are indebted to Dr. Martin Eidelberg, Nancy A. McClelland, the people in the 20th Century Decorative Arts Department at Christie's, and St. Martin's Press for their assistance and hard work in making *Behind the Scenes of Tiffany Glassmaking* a reality so that another side of the Favrile story can be told.

We would also like to recognize Marjorie Nash Carhart for passing on to us the original manuscript and other archival material with the request that we endeavor to publish her father's work.

Finally, we would like to pay tribute to our grandfather, Leslie Hayden Nash, for taking time to document many of the facts and stories surrounding some of the finest art glass made in the twentieth century. His insight, coming from a master glass chemist and designer, has helped to fill the void of knowledge surrounding Favrile glass. We are sure that he is happy knowing that his book, as well as his reference materials and many notes, are now in the hands of people who hopefully will make them available for further research.

PETER H. CARHART

THOMAS M. CARHART

W. JAMES CARHART

LOUIS C. TIFFANY (*SEATED AT RIGHT*) AND GUESTS OUTSIDE LAURELTON HALL, OYSTER
BAY, AT THE ANNUAL MEETING OF THE TIFFANY FOUNDATION, MAY 22, 1927. ARTHUR J.
NASH IS STANDING THIRD FROM THE LEFT.

PREFACE

Behind the Scenes of Tiffany Glassmaking is occasioned by the unexpected appearance of a wealth of archival material about Louis Comfort Tiffany and his various business enterprises. Included within this material are a great many manuscripts from the pen of Leslie Hayden Nash, who was directly in charge of many of Tiffany's departments and who rose to the position of production manager. The most significant of these manuscripts is Nash's *Tiffany Favrile Glass,* the 193-page typescript for a book that was never published. In addition, there are many preliminary drafts for portions of his book, as well as additional stories and anecdotes in manuscript form. Then there is a large scrapbook that Nash kept while at Tiffany Furnaces; pasted into it are original drawings for enamels and lamps and clippings from contemporary magazines and catalogues, all profusely annotated by Nash. Other highlights include an important album with photographs of Tiffany's first glass vessels, and two albums devoted to Tiffany's ceramics. Finally, there is a bewildering array of miscellaneous drawings, papers, and photographs. While much of this material comes from Leslie Nash's tenure, a sizable amount comes from the time of his father, Arthur John Nash, who was in charge of the glass division from the very start of Tiffany's Corona glassblowing plant in the early 1890s. Taken as a whole, these documents are of tremendous historic value. They shed light not only on Louis C. Tiffany's glass, pottery, and enameling departments, but also on many other aspects of his richly diverse career. Most important, they offer insight into the working relationship of Tiffany and two of his chief lieutenants.

After the death of Leslie Nash in 1958 and after various attempts by his family to publish *Tiffany Favrile Glass*, this archival material was first stored in a footlocker by his widow, and then passed on to their children, Marjorie Nash Carhart and John William Nash. In 2000, heirs put much of the material up for auction at Christie's, while still retaining a small amount for their respective families.[1] The wealth of this material, only a portion of which is being published here, is particularly surprising because many scholars, collectors, and dealers had been in contact with Leslie Nash in the 1950s. They had interviewed him and had bought most of his collection of glass, but somehow they remained unaware of these important documents and beautiful watercolor renderings. Even though this archival material might not have had much monetary value at the time, its historic value would have been apparent. Yet no one seems to have gotten wind of what was hidden in the footlocker.

In the course of preparing *Behind the Scenes of Tiffany Glassmaking*, we have been befriended by many colleagues and associates, and even if we do not name them here, we want to express our gratitude. Among those whom we would like to mention is Eric Streiner, who generously allowed us to photograph some of the many wonderful objects in his collection. Herb and Sylvia Kornblum also kindly made their collection available to us. We are especially grateful to John

Loring of Tiffany & Co., who kindly permitted us to illustrate certain images from Leslie H. Nash's scrapbook, *Tiffany Favrile Glass & Metal Products*, now owned by the Tiffany & Co. Archives. Likewise, we appreciate the support of Takeo Horiuchi, who allowed us to reproduce the albums of photographs of early glass and pottery. Further thanks are due to Macklowe Gallery, New York, for letting us photograph one of its Tiffany vases.

At so many turns, we were dependent on the goodwill and expertise of many good friends. We are grateful to Alice C. Frelinghuysen of The Metropolitan Museum of Art, New York, for all her help and encouragement. Likewise, we would be remiss if we did not single out Mr. and Mrs. Robert A. Hut, as well as Bruce Barnes and Joseph Cunningham, for their time and effort, and also Arlie Sulka of Lillian Nassau Ltd., New York, who has long had an interest in early Favrile glass. Janet Zapata helped with her great wealth of knowledge about Tiffany enamels, and Dr. Roberta A. Mayer kindly shared her exciting new information about Associated Artists. Roger Dodsworth, Keeper of Glass and Fine Art, Broadfield House Glass Museum, Kingswinford, helped throw light on Arthur J. Nash's career in England. At several critical moments, Dr. Seth A. Gopin gave invaluable technical expertise, which allowed the manuscript to be processed.

For their help in expediting the receipt of photographs, we would like to thank Rachel Brishoual of the Musée des Arts décoratifs, Paris; Linda M. Cagney and Scott Wolff of the Chrysler Museum of Art, Norfolk, Virginia; Jill Thomas-Clark of the Corning Museum of Glass, Corning, New York; Jennifer A. Rennie, Haworth Art Gallery, Accrington, England; Sandra Wiskari and Julie Zeftel of The Metropolitan Museum of Art Photograph Library, New York; Suzanne Modica, Art Resource, New York.

We certainly cannot overlook the wonderful help and enthusiastic support of everyone in Christie's 20th Century Decorative Arts Department. Without the initial work of Lars Rachen and Peggy Gilges, this project would never have taken place. Above all, we must thank Victoria Rodríguez-Thiessen, who spent endless hours organizing the archival matter under discussion, pursuing with great success seemingly lost causes in the libraries, and creating order out of chaos. Likewise, we must single out Colleen Weis for her working seven-day weeks, arranging the photography, and ensuring that this project came to completion. We are indebted to Katharina Sulke, who proofread with care, helped obtain photographs, and kindly volunteered for many onerous tasks.

The Christie's Photo Studio deserves special mention. We are grateful to Judy Kahn, manager of the Photo Studio, for her ease and goodwill in facilitating the never-ending photography and processing. David Schlegel, Martha Stanitz, Chris Linder, and Douglas C. Ho are responsible for many of the wonderful photographs we have included. Image processors Dean Perry, Omar Rawlison, Janis Henderson, and Darryl Cooper also spent countless hours working on this project, and without them, the visual effect of this book would not have been possible. Additional thanks are extended to other colleagues at Christie's, especially Sonja Ganne, Caroline Stark, and Kaori Yoshida for their invaluable assistance in obtaining photographs from various institutions.

At St. Martin's Press, Jennifer Weis skillfully guided the publication forward with great tact, expertise, and patience, despite the grueling schedule.

Lastly, we owe an enormous debt of gratitude to Peter H. Carhart, who provided much of the material presented in *Behind the Scenes of Tiffany Glassmaking* and who continued to search for additional aspects of Nash family history as the project progressed. We hope that he and his brothers will be pleased by this publication.

MARTIN EIDELBERG

NANCY A. McCLELLAND

VIEW OF THE TIFFANY GLASS AND DECORATING COMPANY BUILDING, NEW YORK, C.

1892–1900. COLLECTION OF THE LOUIS C. TIFFANY GARDEN MUSEUM, MATSUE, JAPAN.

PHOTO: CHRISTIE'S INC.

CHRONOLOGY

1848	Louis Comfort Tiffany born on February 18 in New York City.
1849	Arthur John Nash born on November 1 in Shipton-on-Stour, England.
1872	Louis C. Tiffany marries Mary Woodbridge Goddard.
1873	Louis C. Tiffany's earliest experiments in glass.
c. 1875–80	Arthur J. Nash joins firm of Edward Webb, White House Glass Works, in Wordsley, near Stourbridge, England. Becomes manager and chief designer.
1878	Arthur J. Nash marries Fannie St. Clare Taylor.
1879	Louis C. Tiffany & Associated Artists established with Candace Wheeler.
1880	Louis C. Tiffany establishes a partnership with Candace Wheeler as Tiffany & Wheeler.
	Louis C. Tiffany establishes a partnership with Lockwood de Forest as Tiffany & de Forest.
	Louis C. Tiffany establishes a furniture company named L. C. Tiffany & Co.
1881	Tiffany & Wheeler dissolved; Tiffany establishes Louis C. Tiffany & Co., Associated Artists, with Candace Wheeler and William Pringle Mitchell.
	Arthur Douglas Nash born on August 16 near Stourbridge.
1882	Tiffany & de Forest dissolved.
1883	Louis C. Tiffany & Company, Associated Artists, separated into two businesses: Tiffany controls Louis C. Tiffany & Company; Wheeler controls Associated Artists.
1884	Death of Mary Woodbridge Goddard Tiffany, Louis' wife.
	Leslie Hayden Nash born on February 23 near Stourbridge.

1885	Louis C. Tiffany & Company dissolved; succeeded by Tiffany Glass Company.
1886	Louis C. Tiffany marries Louise Wakeman Knox.
c. 1887–90	Arthur J. Nash joins firm of Edward Webb & Sons, Dennis Glass Works, in Amblecote, near Stourbridge.
c. 1890	Arthur J. Nash arrives in the United States.
1892	Arthur J. Nash's family arrives in the United States.
	Tiffany Glass and Decorating Company established on February 18; furnace built in Corona, Long Island; production of Favrile glass under Arthur J. Nash begins.
1893	Stourbridge Glass Company is incorporated on April 7 as a separate entity to produce glass vessels.
	Louis C. Tiffany triumphs with his exhibition at the World's Columbian Exposition, Chicago.
	Stourbridge Glass Company factory destroyed by fire on October 28.
1894	Registration of Favrile glass trademark by Tiffany Glass and Decorating Company on November 13.
1895	Inaugural exhibition at S. Bing's *L'Art Nouveau* gallery, Paris, includes Tiffany's Favrile glass and windows.
1895–97	Collections of Favrile glass go to the Smithsonian Institution, Washington, D.C.; The Metropolitan Museum of Art, New York; and the emperor of Japan, Tokyo.
1897	Bronze foundry and metal shop established at the Corona factory.
1898	Tiffany Glass and Decorating Company absorbs Schmitt Brothers Furniture Company.
1898–99	Enameling department established.
1899	Grafton Galleries, London, exhibits Tiffany lamps, windows, and glassware.
c. 1900	Leslie H. Nash studies art in Europe.
1900	At World's Fair in Paris, Louis C. Tiffany and Arthur J. Nash both awarded grand prizes.
	Tiffany Glass and Decorating Company renamed Tiffany Studios on September 29.
	Pottery department begun.
1901	Tiffany wins grand prize at the Pan American Exposition, Buffalo, New York, and at exhibitions in Dresden, Germany, and St. Petersburg, Russia.
1902	Stourbridge Glass Company is renamed Tiffany Furnaces on September 29.

1902	Allied Arts Company established to include Schmitt Brothers Furniture Company and Tiffany Studios.
	Tiffany Studios showroom relocated to 45th Street and Madison Avenue.
	Tiffany awarded a grand prize at the International Exposition of Modern Decorative Art in Turin, Italy.
	Louis C. Tiffany appointed design director of Tiffany & Co. upon the death of his father, Charles Lewis Tiffany.
c. 1904	Tiffany Studios begins to produce jewelry.
1904	Tiffany awarded gold medal at Louisiana Purchase Exposition, St. Louis, Missouri.
	Laurelton Hall, Louis C. Tiffany's summer home near Oyster Bay, Long Island, completed.
1906	Leslie H. Nash works as an engineer for the Pennsylvania Railroad tunnels under the East River in New York City.
1908	Leslie H. Nash employed full-time by Tiffany, assuming control of the blown glass department and eventually managing the pottery and enameling departments.
1910	Leslie H. Nash marries Bessie (Betty) Dennett James.
	Louis C. Tiffany awarded gold medal at the Paris Salon.
1911	Mosaic fire curtain for the National Theater, Mexico City, is exhibited in New York.
1912	Leslie H. Nash assigned responsibility for the window glass department by Arthur J. Nash.
1913	Egyptian fete held at Tiffany Studios, 345 Madison Avenue, to commemorate Louis C. Tiffany's sixty-fifth birthday.
1914	Tiffany awarded honorable mention at Salon des artistes français, Paris.
	Publication of Charles de Kay's *The Art Work of Louis C. Tiffany.*
1915	Louis C. Tiffany awarded gold medal at Panama-Pacific Exposition, San Francisco, California.
	The Dream Garden mosaic mural, produced by Tiffany Studios from a design by Maxfield Parrish for the lobby of the Curtis Publishing Company building, Philadelphia, is exhibited in New York.
1916	Retrospective of Tiffany's work held at Tiffany Studios to celebrate Louis C. Tiffany's sixty-eighth birthday. "Quest for Beauty" pageant held.
1919	Louis Comfort Tiffany Foundation created to aid gifted young artists.
1920	Tiffany Furnaces reincorporated as Louis C. Tiffany Furnaces, Inc., on January 6.
1921	Tiffany awarded Place of Honor gold medal at the Paris Salon.

1924   Louis C. Tiffany Furnaces, Inc., dissolved; A. Douglas Nash Company created on April 2.

1928   Leslie H. Nash advised by Tiffany & Co. that no more iridescent glass will be sold.

c. 1929   Establishment of L. H. Nash Metal Arts.

1929   On October 24, "Black Thursday," stock market crashes.

c. 1929–30 A. Douglas Nash Company closes.

1932   Tiffany Studios, then under the direction of Joseph Briggs, files for bankruptcy on April 16.

1933   Death of Louis Comfort Tiffany on January 17.

1934   Death of Arthur John Nash on March 13.

1936   Tiffany Studios' remaining inventory sold to auctioneer Percy A. Joseph of New York.

1938   Death of Fannie St. Clare Taylor Nash, Arthur J. Nash's widow.

            Auction of the residue of the stock from Tiffany Studios held by Lester Dutt and Associates, Washington, D.C.,
            March 14–19.

1940   Death of A. Douglas Nash on March 31.

1946   Tiffany Foundation sells contents of Laurelton Hall at Parke-Bernet Galleries, New York, on September 24–28.

1957   Fire largely destroys Laurelton Hall.

            Leslie H. Nash completes manuscript of *Tiffany Favrile Glass.*

1958   Death of Leslie Hayden Nash on February 9.

1959   Death of Betty Dennett James Nash, Leslie H. Nash's widow.

ARTHUR J. NASH. PHOTO: CHRISTIE'S INC.

ARTHUR J. NASH

Arthur J. Nash's importance to Tiffany's glassmaking operations has been increasingly recognized in the last few decades, yet we have known curiously little about the man. We have lacked most of the basic facts of his life and career. We had no likeness of him, much less any sense of his character. Now, through various documents in the Nash archives, we can establish something of his life. His son Leslie, anxious to record his father's achievements and to gain for him the recognition that he believed Tiffany had stolen, composed some thoughts on paper. As was his custom, Leslie first wrote out several drafts in longhand. Three such essays have come down to us. The first two are incomplete sketches. The next, a more complete study, is by repute the sixth writing. The last item is, in essence, a postscript. Although all three biographies are somewhat repetitious, nonetheless, together they tell us a great deal about Arthur Nash (and, at the same time, about his son). But, as will quickly be evident, these three accounts need to be both supplemented and carefully scrutinized. There are major gaps in the telling of the story, and some of the "facts" need to be interpreted.

ARTHUR J. NASH[2]

To the best of my knowledge and memory. I was rather young while these things were going on.

Qualifacations

Born Stratford in Avon—

He was an only son brought up by a severe father who did not spare the rod, an English tradition of the way to bring up boys[3]

While his father was not a minister he was an ardent Bible student and M Nash was brought up in a severe way—he taught Sunday school—sang in a quire gave readings from Shakespeare and attended all services in the church—he secured his education in the best schools England had to offer—he majored in glass chemistry—acted as consulting chemist for glass factories in England and read many papers on industrial chemistry very fond of walking—a graduate of the Academy of Fine and Applied Art—his hobby was steel engraving. He also invented many processes for etching on metal and worked in vitreous enamels—

He married Fannie St. Clare Taylor whose father built the first steel building in London—had six children two died very young—the surviving, Percy—Douglas—Leslie and Gerald—

My mother was a consert singer trained for Grand Opery—a fine musitian—

My Father gave penny readings for the very poor children at the Town Hall in Birmingham and London every Sunday afternoon for twelve years— the money provided food and clothing for the very poor

[page missing]

one was drawn steel tubing for the Humber Bycycle Co—He gave the information to his brother in law—who made a large sum of money. However my Father always wanted to make glass—and became associated with Edward Webb who was starting a glass factory in Stourbridge England he became a partner.

Mr Webb gave little time to business; he prefered hunting and social affairs and finally was Knighted and became Sir Edward. I have no further knowledge about Sir Edward.

About 1890 the glass business in England was on a downward trend—and Father sensing trouble decided to come to America.

Through a mutual friend of Mr Tiffanys and Father—a Mr Gerald M Stanton an American who spent much time in England stayed at our house many times—he told Father about Mr Tiffany and a meeting was arranged after coming to US—Father wanted to visit two old friends of his Mr Sellers McKee and Mr Libby—this he did M^r McKee wanted Father to come to Pittsburgh and run the factory but it was a comercial product Dad prefered Art glass so desided to see what Tiffany wanted—after one or two experiments in a Boston—to prove his ability. It was then that the factory built under Fathers direction brought into being the now honored Favrile glass.

MY FATHER

Born in England came to US 1892

While I write, the greatness of my Father comes to me.

"Walk by faith and not by sight" I think, when Dad looked at the many beautiful things we made. He saw beyond their entrinsic value as an object of trade. it was more the thought, that these things would bring happyness into the lives of others—in some strange way. To gain this ultimate beauty made him work only the harder—

I was always conshus that the guarded statements to people—contained something most people found it difficult to understand.

He had a profound understanding of things good—and by his faith, removed many obstacles.

For twelve years he gave Penny readings to the very poor children in Birmingham England and every now and then in London—

The stories he read were geared to their age—but he somehow always got round to something from the Bible—many times he could fill the Town Hall. The pennies clothed and fed the very poor.

This is the type of man, in my mind that should be recognized. He never made mention of his accomplishments. This I should try to do—over the family moto—"Omnia Vincit Veritas"

MY FATHER ARTHUR J. NASH

First of all, may [I] say that in discribing him, I shall touch on his qualifications pertinent to the manufacture of glass, and his coming to America, his meeting Louis Tiffany and the forming of the company which made the now famous glass called "Favrile". Mr. Nash has had a distinguished career.

In a few lines, I will try briefly to give you a bit of his background.

First of all he was dedicated to the teaching of the Bible—having been brought up by a strict father. His early training was devoted to church work. For twelve years he gave penny readings to the poor children of Birmingham and London The money collected was used to provide food and clothing for those without anything.

Mr. Nash also gave readings from Shakespeare and could talk on almost any subject.

He was well educated in the best English schools—and made chemistry his major subject which was applied to the manufacture of glass.

He was a consultant on glass for many English manufacturers, and lectured on industrial chemistry. He invented many new things. He was definitely a mans man. After experimenting for a short time in Art metal work, and had developed a method for drawn steel tubing for the Humber bycycle works; desided to go into glass, his first love. He was introduced to Edward Webb in Stourbridge who was just starting a glass works. They formed a partnership—called The Whitehouse Glass Works—which after some years changed to Thomas Webb & sons. The marking on their glass was a cobwebb.

Edward Webb was a sportsman and spent much time hunting and moved about in social affairs; he let Dad run the business almost entirely. he was knighted, which gave him the title Sir Edward Webb—the glass business from an Art standpoint—was loosing ground fast all over England. Father seeing this, decided to come to US had two English friends in the U.S., Mr. Sellers McKee and Mr. Libby [crossed out: "who spent much time in England and was"], both in the glass business. Mr Gerald M. Stanton a mutual friend of Father and LCT an American who made many trips to England, told father of LCT's efforts in church windows but could not get the colors he desired.

Mr Stanton saw Mr Tiffany on his return to US and Mr Tiffany who had hurd about Dad for some time, wrote to Father and asked him to call on him if he came to US. Father decided to visit McKee and Libby in America. One was Sellers McKee mentioned above who wanted Father to manage his glass business but Dad thought it was to comercial and refused the offer. Father after an interview joined with Louis Tiffany, which brought about Favrile glass,—and a company was formed and a factory was built at Corona LI NY—under the name Tiffany Glass & Dec Co. This Mr. Nash did not like—and decided to form his own Co called the Stourbridge Glass Co later change three times Tiffany Furnaces Inc. then LC Tiffany Furnaces Inc. and last Louis C. Tiffany Furnaces Inc.[4]

There were many occasions when I overheard Mr Tiffany asking Father to give more detail on glass formula—but while Dad gave the reaction of many chemicals—he never gave the actual formula on anything pertaining to glass.

Mr Tiffany was disturbed over this—and employed Dr MacKiney, an analitical chemist who came to the factory almost every week with Mr Tiffany. he asked me many questions about glass, thinking that, being young I would give him a bit of information here and there, that when put together would give him the information he was after. I smelled a rat, and spoke to Dad and asked him about Dr Mac as he was called; Dad said no information. Mr Tiffany put him on the Board of Directors—but I never heard him say one word. I always felt that he was a sort of stool pigeon. he was a clever man in his line—which put the Nash contingent on guard. he was finally dismissed—and died shortly after in disgrace. There was never any doubt in my mind that if Dads knowledge could be pumped out of him—he would not remain very long. this was just wishful thinking on somebody's part.

There was one thing for shure. Mr Nash must be kept down in every way, because Dad had received seven gold medals personally.

One only has to read the five changes in the name of our business—to see how carefully the plan of eliminating the name of Nash was carried out. I often thought about this, and was disgusted when the impact of the plan became a fact.[5]

This thing made me put my name on every design I ever I made. They are all in my scrapbook for many years.[6]

AN AFTER THOUGHT

After delving into my note books and articles written over the years during my association with the Tiffany Furnaces, the thought has come to me: Wood my Father approve of the things I have written about.

My Father was a retiring person and praise and honors never interested him to any extent; he seldom talked about such things. He would rather have the opinion of the public at large, rather than three or five jurists.

You can send to Washington to the patent office—and you will find very little on my Fathers inventions. I asked him about this.

He said, to patent any thing is to tell the world. This is especially true when it comes to formulas.

He was a great reader and student and could talk on almost any subject and paid little attention to small talk—Rubish was a favorite remark of his.

In his work, he never left a stone unturned to find the answer.

He was always very good to me, due partly to my loss of sight in one eye, which proved to be a handicap when trying to read. He helped me for many years, reading to me, during my student days. Well I think he would approve my writing about our glass. Because he loved it so much.

As can be seen, the content of Leslie Nash's accounts of his father's life is curiously put forth. These accounts are of great interest because they are so highly personal in their approach, but there is all too little of Arthur Nash's basic biographical statistics, and they barely consider his most important achievements.

To begin with, Leslie neglects to discuss the circumstances of his father's birth. Arthur Nash was born on November 1, 1849, the son of the miller Jesse Nash and his wife Elizabeth Hayden. His birthplace of Shipton-on-Stour, near Stratford-on-Avon, was fitting because, according to family tradition, a Nash ancestor (originally "Attenash") married Shakespeare's granddaughter (or, alternatively, niece). In 1878, Arthur Nash married Fannie St. Clare Taylor, an accomplished singer, and they had six children: Percival Brett, Arthur Douglas, Leslie Hayden, Gerald Lawrence Watson, Norman Corbett, and a daughter, Mabel, who died while the family was still in England.

That Arthur Nash first worked in the metal business comes somewhat as a surprise because there was no hint in previous histories that he had any experience other than in the glass industry. However, as we learn from an earlier typed version of this section, his wife's "father was in the Iron and Steel business and constructed Useton [Euston] station in London, one of the first steel structures to be built in England." Also, Leslie's claim that his father had been a partner of Edward Webb is equally surprising, since he has generally been described as merely a manager.[7] As will be seen, Leslie had a tendency to aggrandize his and his father's achievements.

Not present in these tellings but embedded in a previous, typed version is Leslie's description of his father's appearance and temperament. This is a welcome addition because all too often we lose sight of the man himself:

> Dad was a member of the British Schools and University Club, The National Arts Club, The Transportation Club and many others of less importance. He was a temperate man, loved an English chop and a glass of ale and a few pals to tell a yarn or two. He rose early, took a warm bath following with a cold shower, of ruddy complexion and of fine posture. He was wonderful at fencing and boxing and used to take us boys on at the drop of a hat.[8]

One of the interesting questions is how Arthur Nash came to work for Louis C. Tiffany. The tentative liaison with Edward Libbey, who had just moved his glass factory to Toledo, Ohio, is fascinating new information. Contrary to the story Leslie tells here, in *Tiffany Favrile Glass* he writes that his father and Tiffany were brought together by A. V. Rose, the man who headed the china and glass departments at Tiffany & Co.; this also has a certain logic because Webb glass was sold at Tiffany & Co. Indeed, the two explanations are complementary.

The elder Nash apparently went to the United States ahead of his family and took charge of Tiffany's glass operations on a trial basis. This apparently took place in Boston and perhaps also in a former laundry building in Brooklyn.[9] Having proved himself, Nash then began the planning of a new factory in Corona, a small town on Long Island opposite midtown Manhattan. The exact nature of Arthur Nash's business relation to Tiffany remains problematic. That the new firm was named the Stourbridge Glass Company in deference to Arthur Nash's previous work in England suggests something of Nash's eminence and influence. Leslie Nash seems to side with his family's often expressed opinion that Arthur Nash not only was a partner but actually owned the glass factory in Corona.[10] Various papers of incorporation, however, suggest that, at best, Arthur Nash owned a minor share of the company's stock. A clue to their business arrangements is found in a preliminary draft of "The Last Page" for Leslie's book. There Leslie describes what happened to Arthur Nash after the destruction of the first Corona factory in a fire, "wiping out his entire investment—and then realizing that the refinancing of the Company brought about a condition where he lost control from a partnership—to a man who gained control by a small margin." On several other occasions, Leslie wrote of his father having invested his capital in the building of the first factory, and this would also explain why Arthur, upon seeing the factory wall crash to the ground, exclaimed, "There goes my last dollar."

The documentary evidence shows that at two points in its early history, on June 26 and September 13, 1893, the Stourbridge Glass Company sought financing by issuing additional stock. It was then that Louis C. Tiffany's father became a stockholder and Louis himself was designated as president. All this happened before the fire, which occurred on October 28, 1893. In short, it was not the fire that caused Nash to lose control; rather, it was that only Tiffany, through access to his father's great financial resources, could supply the much-needed capital. Indeed, looking back, when the

Stourbridge firm was first incorporated in April 1893, Nash owned only one share, whereas Tiffany's associates owned the preponderant balance.[11] Even Leslie's assertion that the firm was created when Arthur Nash "decided to form his own Co" seems an unwarranted characterization.

The new contract also limited Nash's artistic control. There apparently was a phrase that gave Louis C. Tiffany artistic control. The story appears in an early draft of Leslie's book: "There was one little catch in my Fathers contract—lets call it the fine print. It read something like this 'It is to be clearly understood that no person or persons shall at any time prepare Glass Batches for melting in the furnaces, without my consent. Should this occur it is understood that I sever my connection with the firm,' or words to that effect. This agreement was signed by L. C. Tiffany." In other words, it was Tiffany and not Nash who got artistic control. Until then, Louis C. Tiffany's name had not appeared on the company's documents, but suddenly he was listed as president.[12]

Leslie's explanation that his father did not like the name Tiffany Glass and Decorating Company and instead formed the Stourbridge Glass Company seems spurious. The scenario he describes in *Tiffany Favrile Glass* has a slightly greater ring of truth—namely, the creation of the two companies with separate names was due to Arthur's wish to separate the blown Favrile vessels from the flat window glass department. But as we now realize, this separation of departments may also have been due to the refinancing and the way in which Tiffany assumed control over all his departments. The lesson to be learned here is that Leslie often skewed the story or claimed more than was the Nash family's proper due as a means of overcompensation for the wrongs—with some justification—he felt had been done.

Arthur Nash, who by everyone's account was directly in charge of all aspects of the glassmaking, held the office of vice-president in 1902, when there was yet another corporate reorganization and the name of the Stourbridge Glass

PHOTOGRAPH OF A GLASSBLOWER AT TIFFANY FURNACES. COLLECTION OF THE LOUIS C. TIFFANY GARDEN MUSEUM, MATSUE, JAPAN. PHOTO: CHRISTIE'S IMAGES, NEW YORK 2000

Company was changed to Tiffany Furnaces. Various reports tell how Tiffany came into the studio with ideas for color combinations in freely rendered watercolor sketches. Because Tiffany had no hand in the actual fabrication of the glass, it was left to Nash to bring these ideas to fruition. That was the essential core of their working relationship. But apparently even the senior Nash did not have any skills at glassblowing; rather, his talent lay in the fabrication of the glass, the development of new techniques, and the supervision of the professional glassblowers.[13]

If Leslie's text is not always entirely reliable, still it offers insights of great importance. His description of Arthur Nash's coded formula books has the ring of truth, and elsewhere Leslie describes reading this coded notebook.[14] While it is not unusual for glassmakers and ceramists to jealously guard their formulas, it is striking to think that Nash kept the secret formulas from even Tiffany, and that Tiffany tried to ferret out these secrets by having his chemist spy.

It should be noted that the chemist whom Leslie remembers as "Dr. MacKinney" was Dr. Parker C. McIlhinney (1870–1923), the man who served as Tiffany's chemist and collaborator and who, until now, has generally been credited with creating the formulas needed in the glass, enamel, and other departments. He was a minor shareholder, and other former Tiffany employees reported that McIlhinney was deeply involved in the fabrication of the glass, especially its iridescent effects.[15] He was also very much involved in the enamel department and later still in the jewelry department at Tiffany & Co.[16] The reason that Nash calls him a "stool pigeon" and the reasons for his dismissal and disgrace are explained in a shocking marginal note that Nash scribbled on a copy of a letter from Frederick Carder, which is in the Nash estate: "Fred Carder an old friend of fathers—was having lunch with Dʳ Ilhiney which started a law suit. Mᶜ Ilhiney was fired from T & Co Tiffany Furnaces and Tiffany Studios He died from disgrace—after being found out that he sold information to Carder."[17] However accurate or not Leslie's account may be, it affords a fascinating insight into the glassworks and the tensions that existed between staff members.

Although Leslie Nash did not write here about the later portion of Arthur Nash's career, elsewhere he tells us that his father relinquished control of the production of the flat glass in about 1912, and that Leslie took control of the production of glass vessels some years later. Apparently Arthur Nash continued to work with Tiffany Furnaces and then with its successor, the A. Douglas Nash Company. Leslie reports that when the Depression struck, Arthur Nash poured money into the failing company in a vain attempt to keep it afloat, but to no avail. Impoverished and in poor health in the last three years of his life, he died a broken man shortly after Tiffany's death.[18]

PHOTOGRAPH OF LESLIE H. NASH, 1930. ESTATE OF LESLIE H. NASH. PHOTO: CHRISTIE'S INC.

LESLIE H. NASH

Whereas Leslie Hayden Nash took great pains to record his father's achievements, he was curiously remiss in preparing his own autobiography. He left us only one very brief essay, which fittingly is subtitled "Just the High Spots." It is a strangely conflated account that gives us some details about his early career before joining Tiffany, barely discusses his work with Tiffany, and almost entirely neglects the next twenty-five years of his life. As frustratingly empty as it may be, this sketch nevertheless provides a convenient starting point for trying to reconstruct his life.

L. H. NASH—A BIT OF MY HISTORY

JUST THE HIGH SPOTS-

At 8 years of age I arrived in USA with my family in 1892

Education Grammar School—High School—Fairchilds Institute

Studied Art in Europe—1900. back to US—refused by Cornell U. loss of sight in right eye, reading poor.

went to work with Franklin Engineering Co. Consulting Engineers. Continued studdies Columbia tutor. Worked on many jobs Refrigeration Electrical work building—and architectural work—Made first Electrical Catalogue for electric supplies 600 pages for Manhattan Electric Co—Elec contracting Mgr. Keystone Elec Co Hotel and Hospital work. All these companys failed. I then went with S Pearson & Co assistant to Mr Mantor [?] Second Eng in charge of PRR East River Tunnels Contract. got touch of the bends and had to quit.

Asked by Dad to go over Glass works and recomend necessary changes in Elec work—during the time at the factory—I built an elec fountain made from large pieces of rock crystal bought by Mr Tiffany we had a carload in the yard—What I did with this rock crystal interested Mr Tiffany so much that he sent for me; and in his studio, he asked me to work permanently at the factory, which I did—in 1908—worked in all departments[19] and finally became Production Manager of all departments—married in 1910—and lasted until the depression almost 23 years with Tiffany which closed the Co. I then lectured on glass, painted and have been teaching art up to the present time.

I am at present finishing a book on the history of Tiffany Favrile glass—Founder member of the Art League of LI—President for 7 years—3½ terms Mrs. Wolcott taken ill—I finished her term of President

In his autobiographical account, Leslie neglects to inform us that he was born in a town outside of Stourbridge in 1884 and was one of Arthur and Fannie Nash's six children.

His memory of life in England, as he recorded elsewhere, was extremely pleasant, and then at the age of eight, he went with his family to the United States. He apparently was not trained to follow his father into the glass industry. Although interested in other aspects of art (studying design and painting in England and France for eighteen months), he was destined for a career in engineering. (It should be remembered that his father and other members of his family had worked in the metals industry.) Thus, Leslie's first positions were with a number of New York City firms, which in one way or another were associated with engineering. The turning point in his early career occurred in June 1906 when he was working for a company engaged in building the Pennsylvania Railroad tunnel under the East River. An explosion killed several of the workmen and left others trapped. Leslie Nash was released after 51 hours, but suffered decompression bends.

One can well understand why Leslie then sought different employment, and it was almost inevitable that he found a position with Louis C. Tiffany's firm. His father had already brought two of his other sons into the business. Arthur Douglas Nash was charged with the distribution of the Tiffany glass to the various representatives, and ultimately became a partner, rising to the position of secretary and treasurer. Another son, Percival Brett, was also briefly involved in the activities of Tiffany's firm. Leslie's description of the incremental stages by which he entered Tiffany's sphere has the ring of authenticity—first on the electrical wiring at the factory, then working on a fountain with "large pieces of rock crystal." The latter undoubtedly refers to the celebrated dragon fountain, which contained rock crystals and was installed in the garden of Tiffany's own home, Laurelton Hall; any engineer working on it would have caught Tiffany's eye.[20]

Curiously, Leslie devoted more lines to his first positions than to his work at Tiffany's factory. According to his own testimony elsewhere, in late 1908 he assumed control from his father of the blown glass department. Gradually, he was charged with other domains including the pottery and enameling departments. In 1912, his father ceded to him the window glass department. With Tiffany's gradual withdrawal from the business in 1919, more changes were engendered. On January 6, 1920, the firm was reincorporated as Louis C. Tiffany Furnaces, Inc. Tiffany was still president, but most of his shares were transferred to the charitable foundation for artists that he had set up in his name. As a result, the Nashes—Arthur J., A. Douglas, and Leslie—owned a large block of the stock and thus had a major role in running the company.[21]

On April 2, 1924, the firm underwent a significant change when it was renamed the A. Douglas Nash Company. Leslie wrote that they made glass for only one and a half years, which would mean that the firm stopped by 1927. However, other indications suggest that it continued until 1929.[22] Elsewhere, Leslie described the demise of the company in the context of the Depression, though without citing a specific year:

> A Directors meeting was called—the auditors read the statement—which showed [us in the red more than (?)400.000]—a very heavy loss. It was voted to go into voluntary bankruptcy. Mr Tiffany bought in all the stock at par, paid all outstanding indebtedness—and the famous Glass business was closed forever—which brought on my Fathers illness from which he never recovered—he passed on in his 86th year.—Shortly following, the Tiffany Studios with all its departments did the same thing.[23]

This would suggest that the factory closed circa 1929–30.[24] Indeed, A. Douglas Nash himself moved to Toledo, Ohio, in 1931 and joined the staff of the Libbey Glass Company, the very same glasshouse that had tried to hire his father a half century earlier.

Just as A. Douglas Nash remained with the glass side of the business, so Leslie chose the metal side. Curiously, though, he started his own firm, L. H. Nash Metal Arts, as early as June 1929.[25] In retrospect, the decision to move in this direction

was sensible because he had had much experience in this area. Moreover, the reliance on etched, stamped, and cast decoration suited the practical side of his businessman's personality. His firm's printed catalogues and his preliminary sketches suggest a wide variety of decorative projects that were closely related to his work at Tiffany Furnaces. His factory was located at 33–24 57th Street in Woodside, Queens, but he also maintained a Manhattan showroom in the Life Building. Little is known about the course of Leslie Nash's company, but it apparently was not long-lived.

In the years after World War II, Leslie Nash spent much of his time as an amateur painter, ironically following the path that Tiffany took in his last years; he also taught others. Forever bringing his organizational skills into play, Nash helped to found the Douglaston Art League, where he served several terms as president. He occasionally lectured on glass and, as his archives suggest, spent a great deal of time reading and copying the history of glass manufacture. Not least of all, he spent many hours writing the story of his days with Tiffany; he finished the manuscript in 1957, the same year that Laurelton Hall was destroyed by fire. Early the next year, on February 9, 1958, Leslie Nash died just a few days short of his seventy-fourth birthday.

Ultimately, Leslie Nash saw himself as having a quite different personality from Tiffany. This is revealed in a marginal note that Leslie penciled in his large scrapbook:

> I hate myself every time I look in this book. LCT is really a pretty fine chap—and is devoted to art. But having worked at engineering and coming in contact with tough men under the East River— played football & golf—my make up—prevented me from understanding a man soft—pampered by everybody. All yes men, but not me. I was used to men—and preferred to be that way—[26]

Leslie's nostalgic looking back to those halcyon days when he worked in a rough-and-tumble world of construction men summons up an American spirit that we associate with Teddy Roosevelt and the Rough Riders.[27] His previous description of his father as "definitely a mans man" tells us much about Leslie.[28] He was the practical businessman who knew how to achieve Tiffany's aesthetic dreams. His designs, especially for the glass that was produced after he assumed control, remind us of the more commercial attitude he generally took and for which he was frequently criticized, even within the firm.

Although Leslie worked closely with Tiffany, it was an intense love-hate relationship. He certainly was not a content employee. Well after the fact, Leslie wrote poignantly sad notes in the archival material he had retained. In the margin of his 1914 contract with Tiffany Furnaces, he wrote, "When I received this I was ready to quit before I started."[29] Alongside a design for an enameled vase labeled "Gold Medal," Nash added, "I would like to get a tin medal."[30] One of his frequently voiced complaints was about a Christmas present he received from Tiffany which he deemed too meager:

> The reason Mr Tiffany failed in business is because he had no love for anyone but Louis C. Tiffany. After twenty five years of hard work he gave me a potted plant for Christmas. Knowing that two exhibitions gave him a gold medal for work he never had seen or had any thing to do with. I personally designed and made the glass in peacock green luster, my invention, and known only to me. One more potted cherry tree for Christmas . . . [31]

First and foremost among Leslie's grievances was his lack of public recognition. Tiffany's publicity stressed one name and one name alone: Louis C. Tiffany. His technical experts and foremen, his artists and artisans, were never mentioned by name. Leslie chafed that he and his father had been grossly neglected while Tiffany basked in the public acclaim. His later notations at the side of a 1913 article about Tiffany discredit the innovations attributed to the master with such pithy remarks as "Bunk No such thing." In response to the printed statement that Tiffany was carrying out his own ideas and his own methods, Nash responded, "I was making flat glass at this time and never received any chemical advice from LCT then or later."[32] Nash felt thwarted, and thus he often overcompensated. His emotional anguish is revealed in his essay about his father, where he thought he discerned a purpose in the frequent name changes of Tiffany's businesses; he saw it as a "plan of eliminating the name of Nash." While it is true that Tiffany frequently changed the names of his companies, both before and after the Nashes joined, the Nash family name was never part of any corporate name until after Tiffany's retirement.

Leslie's retribution against Tiffany's supposed injustices was equally strange: "This thing made me put my name on every design I made. They are all in the scrapbook I kept for many years." Unfortunately, Nash was thorough in signing every design: a large number of them, especially the watercolors for enamels, had been made years before Leslie Nash had even joined the firm, yet he did not hesitate to add his signature ex post facto.

This brief biographical sketch establishes certain fundamental points. Not only did Leslie Nash know stories about Tiffany's earlier years from his father, but he had also been at the center of Tiffany's company in its later years. Thus, he understood in an intimate way the day-to-day operations of Tiffany's enterprises and was in a position to pass this information on to us. On the other hand, given his bias, his report must be scrutinized carefully at every turn.

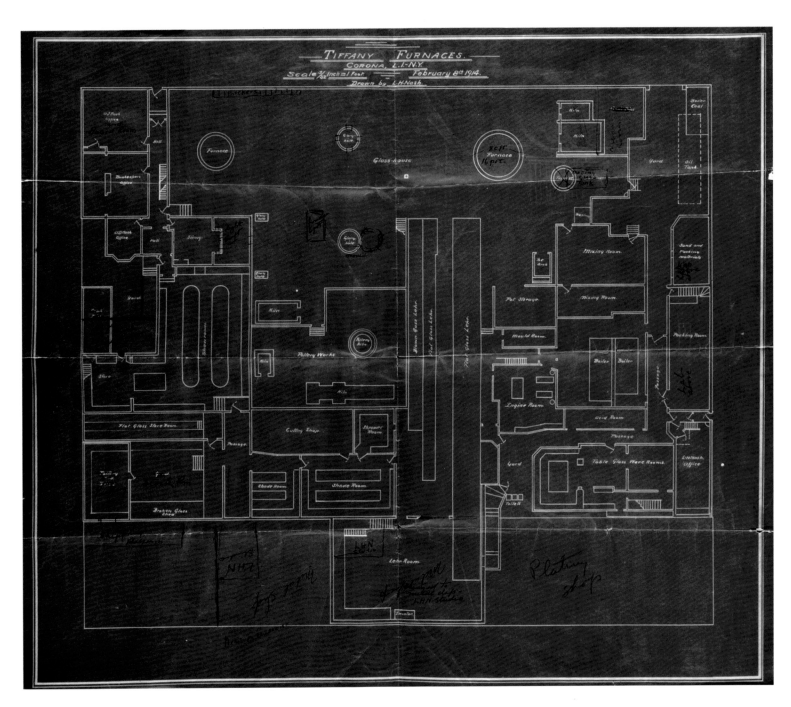

BLUEPRINT OF THE TIFFANY FURNACES FACTORY, CORONA, NEW YORK, DRAWN BY
LESLIE H. NASH, FEBRUARY 8, 1914. COLLECTION OF THE LOUIS C. TIFFANY GARDEN
MUSEUM, MATSUE, JAPAN. PHOTO: CHRISTIE'S INC.

PROLOGUE TO LESLIE H. NASH'S *TIFFANY FAVRILE GLASS*

Throughout his long career, Louis Comfort Tiffany was in the limelight. As a painter, he rarely caught the critics' attention, but by the time he turned to the decorative arts, he recognized the value of publicity and how to obtain it. Articles about the interiors he designed were placed in important journals in the 1880s, and these had the desired effect: Tiffany quickly became a central figure in the art world of New York. His dramatic displays at the Chicago World's Fair of 1893 and the splendiferous palace he created for Henry O. Havemeyer in New York City established him as perhaps the major figure in American decorative arts at that time. Through promotional material that his company generated, through exhibitions in which he participated, and through displays staged in his own galleries, he made his name known not only in this country but also throughout Europe. As he successfully ventured into new media—glass vessels, lamps, bronzes, enamels, ceramics, and jewelry—his triumphs were quickly reported. With each progressive stage, his ambition was matched by his success, both artistically and commercially.

The all-embracing nature of Tiffany's artistic vision and his business acumen bring to mind the efforts of his English counterpart, William Morris. Indeed, Tiffany was undoubtedly inspired by Morris' groundbreaking efforts. If the analogies between the work of these two men are remarkable, the differences between them are equally telling. Morris was of an older generation, and his taste for the Gothic and the early Renaissance was in marked contrast with Tiffany's preference for exotic, non-Western styles. But even more fundamental is their approach to the process of design. Morris himself took an active role as a craftsman, working out the details of many of the designs, conducting experiments with dyes and printing methods, and weaving on the loom. Tiffany's role, on the other hand, was restricted to a more conceptual level. His ideas about form and color were generally limited to rough sketches. As it was described at the time, "his ideas for decoration and glass were mainly expressed by quick, rough color memoranda that could only be understood or interpreted by the artists who surrounded him."[33] Indeed, such sketches from Tiffany's hand are to be found among Leslie Nash's papers. The important thing, though, is that it was left to technicians to perfect the materials—the glass formulas, the enamels, the glazes. Tiffany's staff worked out the specifics of each design, and it was his workers who actually executed the objects. Although most of the objects that issued forth from Tiffany Studios bore a facsimile of Louis C. Tiffany's personal signature, and although they were the product of his mind and genius, they were not from his hand.

This notwithstanding, the publicity that surrounded Tiffany (and which his firm frequently had a hand in generating) always suggested that the glass was his personal work, that not only did it reflect his personal vision but also that he

himself conducted the experiments and, perhaps, even fabricated the glass. The text prepared for S. Bing's exhibition catalogue at the Grafton Galleries in London suggests something of the fabled aura that was spun around Tiffany:

> For years Tiffany gave himself up to these engrossing researches, and gradually succeeded in making a glass which answered the requirements to a wonderful degree. His great ambition was to employ it in the manufacture of *objets d'art*. . . . he sought to go back to the primitive starting-point, and inaugurate a school, in which the supreme refinement of taste and learned technique should be concealed under the most modest exterior. . . . And in the artist's hands there grew vegetable, fruit, and flower forms . . . he created certain kinds of opaque and opalescent glasses. . . . But Tiffany had no sooner overcome one difficulty than he attacked a fresh problem. . . . And now that he felt he exercised mastery over the material, the idea occurred to him to create by his art, beauties analogous to those which, up till then, had been produced . . . by the fortuitous action of time. . . . the iridescent effects obtained by Tiffany were refined to a supreme degree. . . . Having, at the instance of an amateur friend, sought to produce in coloured glass the peacock in all the glory of his plumage, he saw in this motif a theme admirably adapted to display his skill in glass-blowing—the peacock's feather.[34]

After reading such rhapsodic descriptions, one cannot escape the conclusion that Tiffany was both artist and artisan, an artist blessed both with vision and a technician's professional skill.

Few journals reporting on the work from Tiffany's firm referred to individual members of his staff. Except for some of the designers of his leaded windows, the names of his collaborators and employees generally went unmentioned. In particular, Arthur Nash's name is almost never to be found. In a rare exception—an article on Favrile glass published at the turn of the century—Nash was mentioned fleetingly: "As in everything else, there must be a mind to direct and a hand to execute. The executant in this case is Mr. A. J. Nash, an English glass-master of consummate ability, who has charge of the factory at Corona, Long Island, where the Favrile glass is manufactured."[35] Its barely laudatory manner could hardly have pleased Nash.

Almost nothing of the nature of Tiffany's workshop and its processes is recorded in *The Art Work of Louis C. Tiffany*, the biographical account that Tiffany commissioned and had published in 1914, near the end of his career when he was becoming more retrospective. Tiffany's own presence is so overwhelming that the reader might think that it was an autobiography, even though the actual author was Charles de Kay, a noted writer on the arts who was indirectly related to Tiffany by marriage.[36] Tiffany undoubtedly directed the writing quite closely; perhaps he even dictated parts of it at its inception. It is arranged in a series of chapters, each devoted to one of the media in which Tiffany worked, but none of them except for the chapter devoted to glassmaking mention his collaborators or craftsmen. Even the glass chapter barely departs from the central theme of Tiffany's genius, though it does mention his first glass master, a Venetian named Andrea Boldini, and quickly moves on to Arthur Nash, who is described merely as "a practical glass manufacturer from Stourbridge, England, who supervised the building of the factory."[37] Leslie and Douglas Nash were not mentioned at all. Even though Tiffany's artisans were accustomed to an enforced anonymity, this must have been a particularly galling description to the Nashes.

All of this prepares us, then, for the different approach to Tiffany's undertakings that Leslie Nash took in writing his book *Tiffany Favrile Glass*. His version represents the point of view of a man who saw himself as "the motivating genius in the Tiffany Glass factory,"[38] and who, as we have already noted, believed that he and his father, despite their positions of prominence in Tiffany's operations, had never been given their due credit. Although it is an informal series of anecdotes, it is written with a definite point of view—the desire to correct the record.

Leslie Nash's account is a series of many separate chapters; some are straightforwardly factual, but most are short stories, highly anecdotal in character. Various memorandums—on loose sheets in his files (one of which is dated 1946) and also at the back of the album of photographs of early glass—list the stories that he thought might be appropriate to tell. And, indeed, many of these were incorporated into his final manuscript. On the other hand, Nash knew still other tales that he apparently left untold and that now will eternally pique our curiosity: an experience on the sea, his high-school days, Tiffany's torn pongee suit, one about baby cups, another about "a bit of glass for the old woman." Nash's stories were written over the course of many years. Some parts were already in process by the late 1930s, but the total manuscript was not finished until around 1957.

Nash's book needs to be understood in relation to the time in which it was written. Both the abrupt demise of luxury trades after the great Crash of 1929, as well as the rise of the Art Deco style and the Modernist movement, had contributed to the end of Tiffany's reign. Lustrous, iridescent glasswares and intricately worked metal seemed like emblems of a distant, extinct age. However, this prompted an antiquarian interest, and by the 1940s, Tiffany glass was being collected by a number of amateurs. Articles in praise of the glass appeared in magazines such as *Hobbies* and *An-tiques*, though, of course, they did not mention the Nashes by name.[39] This only intensified Leslie Nash's determination to write his book. Moreover, one of these collectors, Leslie C. Byer, a patent attorney living in Schenectady, New York, contacted Nash in 1944 in search of information, and this stimulated an exchange of facts and stories that only encouraged Nash in his writing. Byer informed Nash that another Tiffany collector, Carroll B. Huntress of New York, was announcing publicly her intent to write a book on their common subject, and one can easily understand Leslie Nash's concerns about her sources of information (Huntress had not contacted him, but had interviewed Sarah Hanley, Tiffany's companion in his later years). Leslie was well aware that unless he finished his book, Arthur J. Nash and his achievements would remain forever hidden. Further interest in Tiffany, and thus further pressure on Leslie, was engendered by the auction of the contents of Laurelton Hall from September 24 to 28, 1946. Though today we lament the sale, it was greeted with joy by Tiffany aficionados because it let loose a flood of otherwise unobtainable examples of his work. Nash, not surprisingly, did not attend. But his writing continued on for another decade, as he rewrote and recopied his stories.

Additional articles and other notices about Tiffany continued to appear, but without any reference to the Nashes.[40] The most significant publication was Gertrude Speenburgh's slim book on Louis Comfort Tiffany and his father, which appeared in 1956.[41] It is significant that Speenburgh had apparently not visited Nash, whereas she interviewed Agnes Northrup, the window designer; Julia Munson Sherman of the enameling department; and surviving members of the Tiffany family. She had even penetrated into the interior of Laurelton Hall. But nowhere in her book did she mention the name of any of the Nashes. Leslie wrote several drafts of a letter to her, pointing out what he considered to be factual errors, but it is uncertain if he ever actually communicated with her. Larry Freeman's book on iridescent glass was published the very same year; a rare exception, it mentioned Arthur Nash as the "man who did much to develop the blown Favrile wares. He is reputed to be the only worker that Tiffany ever allowed to sign his reproductions."[42] This garbled statement could hardly have been salve on the wound. But by that time, Leslie Nash finally believed that his own book was in shape.[43]

In October 1956, an exhibit of Tiffany glass was put on display at the Carnegie Institute in Pittsburgh, and quite expectably, it was a paean to Tiffany's name.[44] Ironically, even though the collection came from A. Douglas Nash, the Nashes were barely mentioned. Arthur J. Nash was cited only once, as having managed the glassworks. Even A. Douglas' work for Tiffany was not described (though Leslie recognized that his brother had designed one of the illustrated vases); all that was mentioned was that A. Douglas received the property after the glassworks closed. Leslie's name did not figure anywhere in this account.

Clearly, though, Leslie must have realized that there was an ever-increasing interest in Tiffany. The tempo of events was becoming more rapid, and the need for Leslie to tell his side of the story was urgent. Indeed, more scholars were beginning to approach him in the course of their research. Albert Christian Revi, who was gathering information for his book *Nineteenth Century Glass*, interviewed various members of the Nash family, including Leslie, and was informed of their contribution to Tiffany's success. Revi must have been a receptive audience, because he later repeated many of Leslie Nash's claims.[45] He was probably the first to report that the Nashes "were responsible for all the designs, glass formulas and decorating techniques." Revi's attentive inquiry must have greatly encouraged Leslie in the production of his manuscript. Also, Leslie corresponded with Robert Koch, who was then writing his dissertation on Tiffany.[46] Not only did he supply Koch with information, but because Koch had an-

nounced he was planning to publish his dissertation, Nash sought advice on how he too could publish his book.[47]

On February 20, 1957, Leslie, having compiled a list of more than twenty-five publishers based in New York City, sent out letters to the first five names. In his letter, he explained something of his relationship to Tiffany and his aims:

I have over the years been making notes for a story about art glass and, in particular, Tiffany Favrile glass in which my father, Arthur J. Nash, and myself played an important part.

Although Mr. Tiffany was a great patron of the arts for which he deserves much credit and although it is his name that appears in most articles about Favrile glass, it is my hope in the stories and anecdotes to bring out the real picture of the people and the efforts that contributed to the position that Favrile glass occupies in the glass world and the general world of Fine Arts. Most of the data published to date has been based on hearsay, since neither did Mr. Tiffany or Mr. Nash give interviews nor did the company itself permit very much publicity of the "behind the scenes" story of the company.

As the last surviving member of the firm which closed in 1929, I feel impelled to tell the story of the company and its famous product, Favrile Glass.

At least one of the publishers—Doubleday & Company—expressed interest in seeing the manuscript, but they turned it down, writing that "it was not of sufficient general interest" for their market.[48] Leslie seems not to have had any success with other prospective publishers.

The moment for a book on Tiffany was never more propitious. Robert Koch was at that instant helping to prepare a Tiffany retrospective exhibition at the Museum of Contempo-

rary Crafts in New York, which, unlike the previous display in Pittsburgh, gained national attention.[49] This exhibition opened on January 24, 1958, just two weeks before Leslie Nash's death.[50] His son John continued to clean up the manuscript and tried in vain to find a publisher. One could well imagine, though, that even a firm interested in publishing a book on Tiffany might well have rejected Nash's manuscript. His many anecdotes, as charming as they may be, do not add up to a whole. Not only is it merely an accumulation of discontinuous stories, but it fails to give a complete picture of the operations of Tiffany Studios and Tiffany Furnaces from the 1890s to their end in the 1930s. The manuscript never explains the origin or development of the many separate departments (blown glass, enamels, pottery, etc.). Nor does it chronicle the landmark events in Tiffany's or the Nashes' careers.

One looks in vain for Nash's account of Tiffany's displays at all the national and international exhibitions, both small and large, where the company presented its wares. There are occasional references to some of the prizes that the Nashes won, but these appear only in relation to Leslie's continued complaint that Tiffany never gave his staff sufficient recognition.

Ironically, Leslie Nash also failed to discuss the individual artisans who contributed to the success of Tiffany's operation. Except for his praise of Frederick Wilson as a designer of leaded windows, he offers no insight into the artistic or personal aspects of these capable workers. In Leslie's day-to-day dealings with his staff, he had apparently a good working relationship. The testimony of the glassblower Jimmy Stewart is pertinent in this regard:

> I want to say that Leslie was a fine boss—he was a fine boss, yes. When he come to you, when he was going to try something, he wouldn't come bulldozing like the majority of bosses do, that I saw and worked for. He'd just say, "Well, Jimmy, we're gonna try something new." *We* are gonna try, not *I*.[51]

Although Leslie Nash wrote at great length of "Joe," the otherwise unidentified night watchman who was burned checking the fuel gauge, and of "Florence," a capable but not gifted officeworker, he did not shed any light on the more important members of the staff. The annotations of the names of the individual glassworkers on some of the company photographs is enlightening, but, it should be remembered, Nash had not intended to include them in his book.[52] Although he provided an invaluable list of all the departments within Tiffany's operation, it is disappointing not to know the names of the heads of each department, the staff of designers, and the craftsmen. It is all the more frustrating when one realizes that he prepared, at least in draft form, just such a list but then dropped the topic. Through the testimony of other Tiffany workers and their descendants, we know some names, but Nash's manuscript, like Tiffany's autobiography, eschews such personal elements.[53]

One might well wonder, then, why Leslie Nash's manuscript is being published now. The answer is that his text offers valuable insights into the history of Tiffany's operation, although often these insights can be gleaned only with a certain effort. For example, his various estimates and recalculations of the date at which glassblowing began at Corona ultimately allow us to establish a relatively secure chronology—namely, that the factory was completed by late 1892 and that glassblowing began in earnest in 1893. Some of the tales that he tells, such as the opposition of the Corona townspeople to the building of Tiffany's factory and the fire that destroyed the plant, were already known but not in such great detail.[54] His discussion of his father's formula books is illuminating: not only does it negate the claim made by A. Douglas Nash's widow that there had been no such formula books,[55] but it also suggests something of the experimentation that went on and the contribution made by Nash to achieve color effects. That the formulas were written in code and the chemicals stored with coded designations alert us to

the tension that existed within the firm, not only due to the fear that workers might steal the formulas and take them to competitors, but also that a veil of secrecy existed between the Nashes and Louis C. Tiffany.

Other stories offer insights into the day-to-day operations of the factory. For example, we know that prior to Leslie Nash's arrival, the company stored some two to three thousand tons of colored glass for the window department, with approximately five thousand different color combinations.[56] What we had not known until reading Nash's text is that there had been no rational system of storing it until he took over. Also, we get some sense of the rivalries between the different departments from his account: how the window department requested new batches of specially colored glass be made for individual projects and how they were charged when they broke panes of glass. This accords with what little has been known about interdepartmental politics and accounting.

Certainly some of Leslie's statements are exaggerated and, in some instances, erroneous. His frequently repeated claim that he and his father created everything in glass, and that Tiffany never had any valuable ideas, appears exaggerated.[57] More than likely, it was Tiffany's personal vision and genius—visible well before the Nashes were in the United States—that was the key to their success. Nonetheless, it is interesting to discover that Nash did win awards at the Paris World's Fair of 1900, as is demonstrated by the photographs of two of the actual diplomas that Leslie intended to illustrate.

Scattered throughout the manuscript are significant insights into the business side of Tiffany's operation. Nash's description of the chaotic storage system for flat glass in the window department and how he reorganized it reminds us of how Tiffany's interests were solely aesthetic, whereas Leslie Nash was more of a rational engineer and businessman. Also, the rivalry that evidently existed between the glass and window departments, and the interdepartmental system of billing show us aspects of Tiffany's operation that have been hidden until now. Likewise, Nash's discussion of Tiffany's foreign trade in small glass items is an interesting insight. So too, his explanation of the numbering system for the glass offers yet more evidence toward the decipherment of Tiffany's registration system.

Nash was not in any sense of the word a trained historian. As is evident by certain sections of his text dealing with older history (English glass, the history of cathedral windows, etc.), it was his custom to borrow such data from other books. This is also apparent in his notes, where one finds much borrowed material of this sort. On the other hand, when it came to writing about Tiffany, he seems to have referred to little if any published material. There are exceptions, of course, as in his lists of Tiffany's prizes, the major commissions for windows, and names of the tableware patterns, all of which are evidently taken from brochures issued by Tiffany. Also, of course, many of the illustrations he planned to include were taken from the various brochures issued by the firm.

On the whole, though, Nash relied heavily on his memory, and thus, ultimately, certain portions of his manuscript are flawed. His citation of names, titles, and dates is not always accurate. In that he did not join Tiffany's operation until late 1908, his discussion of the beginning stages in the 1890s and the turn of the century are based on secondhand infor-mation. Certainly, he must have learned much of this from his father, but while there is a general ring of truth, details may not always be very accurate. For example, while it may well be that in the later years Tiffany went to the Corona plant only on Monday mornings and was indecisive, this may well not reflect the state of affairs fifteen years earlier. Occasionally, there are reasons to doubt Nash's assertions. For instance, one might well wonder whether the two iridescent glass vases in his collection (see page 53) were really made by Arthur Nash in England as Leslie claims, or were made at Tiffany's plant in Corona in the first years.

Curiously absent from Leslie Nash's testimony is the animosity he frequently expressed in earlier drafts of text and in marginal notations on working drawings. Nash frequently railed at how Tiffany had not sufficiently acknowledged the two generations of the Nash family for all they had contributed to his success. Throughout his papers, Leslie told the story of how he had once won a prize for Tiffany at an international fair, and Tiffany rewarded him only with a potted plant at Christmas. None of these charges are reiterated in this manuscript, but Leslie's intent to illustrate two of his father's diplomas from the Paris World's Fair of 1900, and his caption referring to the number of others won by his father can be seen as a partial remedy to this deeply felt injury. In this instance, Nash was extremely tactful about this sore point—one which was felt as well by others within the studio.

NOTE ON THE EDITING OF NASH'S TEXT

In presenting Leslie H. Nash's text, it was necessary to make certain editorial decisions. The overriding philosophy was to present it as close as possible to the state in which Nash left it. Thus, we have not completed incomplete sentences, omitted repetitions, or corrected known errors. Nash's very personal style of punctuation has been retained, as has his use of capitalization for emphasis and his particular form of organizing his paragraphs. Although this means that a great many spelling and punctuation errors have been retained, it also allows us to preserve something of the delightfully forthright flavor of his account.

Leslie Nash's *Tiffany Favrile Glass* was prepared in typewritten form to present to a publisher. It was apparently written over a period of years, and drafts of certain portions are to be found elsewhere among texts the author left behind. The final manuscript, which is dated 1957, was typed in nonsequential stages, as can be seen by the erratic shifts in typeface; some portions were retyped even after the author's death.

To indicate that the original text was typewritten, the text has been set in roman type. Where Nash himself modified his typescript by adding changes in pencil, this has been indicated by setting the changes in italics. Where there were self-evident typos or double typings of words, we have corrected such errors. Where we thought that commentary would be helpful, we have added it, using a conventional endnote system.

Unaccustomed to the realities of publishing, Nash planned his book as a series of small chapters. In the typescript, each section is headed with a title, almost always in capital letters and frequently underlined, and each section begins on a new page. Most sections run for only two or three pages; some are less than a page in length. A printed book, however, can accommodate far more text to a page, and so Nash's scheme of starting each new section on a separate page was abandoned. The titles of his sections, now consistently set in boldface and in capital letters, preserve Nash's intended effect.

Nash chose a great many illustrations to accompany his text, and we have tried to follow his indications as much as was practical. We have attempted to place the illustrations as close as possible to where he indicated. Occasionally, Nash used the same illustration twice, but when this occurred we omitted the second appearance. Where he offered a choice of alternate photos in color as well as black and white, we chose the latter because the color photographs were poor, homemade products whose color had long since faded. We have kept the form of his captions, but have set them entirely in capital letters, whereas Nash occasionally underlined phrases and erratically used lower case as well. We omitted his notes to the hypothetical publisher, in which he discussed the need for copyright permission, etc.; some of his more significant directions have been retained in notes.

MARTIN EIDELBERG

NANCY A. McCLELLAND

24

TIFFANY

FAVRILE GLASS

by

Leslie Hayden Nash[58]

1957

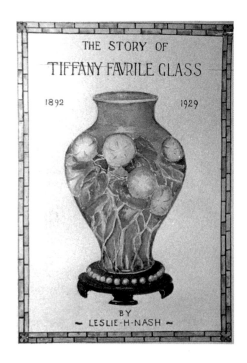

MORNING GLORY GLASS—

WATERCOLOR BY THE AUTHOR

TIFFANY FAVRILE GLASS

PAGE   CONTENTS (CONT.)

PAGE　　　　　CONTENTS (CONT.)

PAGE   CONTENTS (CONT.)

NOTE—THE PICTURES ARE INCLUDED IN THE CONTENTS BECAUSE THEY ARE
CLOSELY RELATED TO THE CONTINU*U*M OF THE BOOK.

WITHOUT THE PICTURES THE BOOK WOULD BE OF LITTLE VALUE.

TO

My late father,

Arthur J. Nash

My wife, Betty, and our children

Marjorie and John

(LEFT) SELF PORTRAIT OF THE AUTHOR. (RIGHT) THE AUTHOR LESLIE H. NASH

ACKNOWLEDGEMENTS

To my brother, Percival B. Nash, for some water colors of early table glass.

To my son-in-law, Clinton P. Carhart, for his assistance in business affairs.

To my son, John Wm Nash, for his photographic assistance in illustrating this book.

Quotations from the Washington Record were brought to my attention by my friend
    Leslie C. Byer, Patent Attourney for General Electric Co.

To my secretary, Pauline Blazek, for her untiring assistance in the typing of this book.

LOUIS C. TIFFANY PRESIDENT. LOUIS C. TIFFANY FURNACES INC. [PAINTED] BY THE AUTHOR

LOUIS C. TIFFANY

The late Louis C. Tiffany was a man dedicated to Art, a painter of high reputation and a member of the National Academy. He was involved in many projects, such as; church windows, Mosaics, rugs, furniture, interior decoration, lighting fixtures, iron work, bronze foundry, granite quarry and many more.

Mr. Tiffany made many trips to Europe and was very fond of Oriental Art. His use of Favrile glass brought him many personal honors.

As for myself, I found Mr. Tiffany a very pleasant and happy person to work with, covering a period of twenty three years. There were only two things we did not agree on, one was perpetual motion and the other was fountains.

As the object of this book is Favrile glass, I shall refrain from further comment on Mr. Tiffany. If further information is desired, see his biography.

Mr. Tiffany died Jan 17ᵗʰ 1933 at the age of eighty-four years.

(LEFT) THE OCTAGONAL COURT TIFFANY RESIDENCE TAKEN ABOUT 1908. THIS RESIDENCE WAS SOLD BY THE TIFFANY FOUNDATION AND THE ENTIRE MANSION WAS DESTROYED BY FIRE IN 1957. (THIS IS A PHOTOGRAPHIC COPY OF COLOR PHOTO MADE BY A. R. RADCLYFFE, IN 1908. ORIGINAL PICTURE APPEARED IN "COUNTRY LIFE IN AMERICA" IN 1908.)

ARTHUR J. NASH

1849–1934 ARTHUR JOHN NASH VICE
PRESIDENT LOUIS C. TIFFANY FURNACES
INC.

Arthur J. Nash was born in England in 1849. He was an only child and his childhood was spent in Stratford-on-Avon.

He received his education in some of the best schools England had to offer. He was a graduate of the Academy of Fine and Applied Arts. During his student years he spent much of his spare time in Museums to study glass and paintings. For a hobby he took up steel engraving and made some exquisite plates, but even more than this, was his interest in chemistry, he specialized in its application to glass. Later this became his life work. There was nothing he did not experiment with in glass. He paid much attention to optical glass and discovered that the presence of iron in any form caused stria (an oily appearance) which was the most destructive thing in the making of optical glass. The waste of material and the preparation of this glass was the cause of his giving it up.

His experiments in the crystalization of glass, leaving the crystals in suspension as you see in a fine opal, were most interesting. It was through these experiments that he discovered luster glass which is explained in his book of formula. He could make almost any color in glass and was called upon by Chances and Powells, English Church Windowmakers, to produce colors which they were unable to develop.

Mr. Nash was well known throughout the European glass industry as an authority in glass chemistry. Due to this knowledge he became associated with Mr. Edward Webb of the Whitehouse Glassworks in Stourbridge, England.[60]

This glass was of a highly artistic nature and received many awards of honor. The marking on the glass was a cobweb.

About the year 1890, imports of cheap glass into England caused a slump throughout the entire glass industry. My father, giving this much serious thought, decided to go to America.[61] He had some close friends in the glass business in the United States, Sellers and McKee and Mr. Libby. Through a mutual friend, Gerald M. Stanton, he was introduced to Louis C. Tiffany, who was looking for a man who could give him a wide range of colors for his windows. Mr. Nash was highly recommended to Mr. Tiffany by Arthur V. Rose, head of the china and glass Dept. in Tiffany & Co., N.Y.

Mr. Tiffany had tried to make glass in a small way but failed and closed his small factory which I think was located in Brooklyn.

Mr. Nash made a few experiments for Mr. Tiffany in a Boston factory rented for this purpose.[62] Everything was satisfactory and a partnership was formed by Louis C. Tiffany and Arthur J. Nash.[63]

In the summer of 1892 Mr. Nash brought his wife and children to the United States, and a factory was built in Corona, Long Island, New York. Mr. Tiffany at first combined the glass manufacture with window making and interior decorating, it was called The Tiffany Glass and Decorating Company.[64]

My Father did not think the combination was wise, so later this Company was reorganized and the glass making became a seperate Company called The Stourbridge Glass Company.[65] Again the name was changed and it finally Became Louis C. Tiffany Furnaces, Incorporated.[66]

Arthur J. Nash was a valuable man and without his knowledge the Tiffany Favrile glass never could have been made.

A. J. NASH MAKES A FEW NOTES
in his book of formulas

Further reading of Dad's books of Formula reveals many interesting notations.[67] I judge the time to be prior to 1888, because at that time he had just finished a glass dress for the Paris Exhibition. Silk *like* threads of various colored glass were woven into a kind of cloth and later fashioned into a ladies dress for which he received high honors. He mentioned it as an experiment.[68]

Another note was the making of glass for signal lights for the British Railway, lighthouse prisms and crystals for beacons and how the Railroad complained of the high price of the ruby glass. He never changed the price and never told that pure gold went into its making.

Luster glass must have been on his mind for many years as his formula shows. Knowing the final formula, one slight change in Dad's would have done the trick and saved him many years of research. He finally discovered his error. I cannot understand why he never put it on the *English* market. I have some samples which show a beautiful example of the use of this now famous glass called FAVRILE.

I checked my own formula with his early *English* experiments and found a slight change. This change came about in the introduction of blue luster. The only other change was made *later* by myself in the production of Peacock green luster. My reward was a gift of stock in the Company and made me a member of the Board of Directors.

It must have been about this time that Dad was experimenting on Moonstone glass. His notes on colored rolling glass went back for many years and I counted no less than 160 various formula covering every shade of color used in church window glass. One more note: "the finer the window, the fewer the colors." In simple words he thought that less confusion in color would not offer such a complex problem.

I believe this is correct because I have seen many paintings ruined by the introduction of too many colors. For my part I have felt from viewing many windows that unity had been lost. I think Dad must have felt the same as we often discussed this problem. A window is often spoiled by being too literal in its rendering, also in color, sudden contrast produced hardness. Heavy lead lines without relation to composition often ruin many windows. *in early windows* This was caused by breakage when firing the colors or stains.

In church I like my mind to be quiet and undisturbed. Some windows give me quite the reverse feeling. Reverence is hard unless you are in a peaceful frame of mind. If the atmosphere is right you benefit more. If you are disturbed by confusion of color and design much of the spiritual side of worship is lost.

The long list of colors made by Mr. Nash was added to by my brother Douglas and myself.

Turning the pages of my fathers books, I find that he gave much time to the study of the lead content of Flint or Crystal glass. He makes note of Irish Waterford glass having heavy content of lead. While the early Waterford was very dark, it's brilliance was rich and beautiful. However, in order to retain it's beauty, it had to be cleaned and polished frequently. My father attributed this to the oxidizing of the accessive amount of lead.

Following this interesting observation, I discovered that he had gone deeply into the study of French Crystal, Belgium Crystal, and many more. Each of those glasses contained a wide variation in the lead content used. But, when the glass pieces were put together, each had a marked differance in color, one a slight tinge of yellow, one gray, one bluish, one colorless, and many more.

It was only after his research on Crystal glass, that he was sent for by other manufacturers, to help them out of their difficulties.

It would prove interesting to note the many color changes in a large collection of cut crystal glass. These color changes are also very noticable in pressed forms that are made of lime glass, without lead.

ENGLISH ORIGIN OF GLASS

"As for glassmakers they be scant in the land
Yet one there is as I do understand,
And in Sussex is now his habitation
At Cheddingsfold he works his occupation."

The first glass plant was established in England and dates back to 1555. Thomas Charnock, the Poet, makes timely mention of it in the above stanza.

Earliest colored glass for optical purposes dates back to 1561.

First Telescope was invented by Leonard Diggs in 1571.

Ruby glass was invented in Potsdam, in 1673, by The Duke of Lanenburg and the secret was held for 200 years. Pure gold was used and his process was discovered by his request for gold coins.

Chinese glass (no mention made).

First plate glass in the year 1771 started at Ravenhead, England. Plate glass made in France was considered best for mirrors.

First Magic Lantern was invented by Phillip Carpenter in England in the year 1808. Lenses made of lead glass.

Bohemian Gold Glass was produced by putting gold fragments between two layers of glass to form a design or just a sprinkled effect. Many glassmakers have tried to produce gold but have failed.

Eye glasses were discovered in the year 1303. The following was found on a tombstone in Florence, Italy:

Here lies

Salvino Armati Armati—Inventor of eye glasses

May God pardon his sins

ENGLISH GLASS

The finest period of English glass was prior to 1890. My Father, Arthur J. Nash had manufactured glass in England through the latter part of this period and gained a high reputation for his contribution in the field of Art glass. His beautiful flint glass is rich, soft and brilliant with a bell-like tone. In all my experience in glass I have never seen a more beautiful crystal. It was not white like the glass you see today. It had depth and quality.

I can see him now smoothing the surface with his hands and running his thumbnail up and down to see if it had received the proper heat during its melting. My father had many awards and compliments for his crystal glass.

Much of this glass could be found on the tables of royalty, engraved with coats of arms, crests, monograms and other devices. I have one goblet in my collection which shows the exquisite design created by my Father in his prime. I doubt if anyone could improve his wonderful composition and use of line. The figure and monogram are high above the standard. (See photograph)

STOURBRIDGE—ENGLAND

A very interesting story is placed at the old Whitehouse Glassworks located at Stourbridge, England, which was my father's factory before coming to the United States

(RIGHT) ENGRAVED GLASS. AN EXAMPLE OF MASTERFUL DESIGNE BY ARTHUR J. NASH.

(FAR RIGHT) THESE THREE PIECES WERE MADE BY A. J. NASH IN ENGLAND. OPAL, LINED, PALE RUBY, DECORATED IN RAISED GOLD COLORS, AN INVENTION OF HIS. THE MARKING IS A COBWEB.

of America. In my childhood I can recall great excitement going on in our beautiful old Georgian home about three miles from the factory.

Mother was busy about the house. I am sure it did not need anything because English homes in those days were a finished product, like most of our American homes today. In the drawing room, which was furnished with gilt and brocade furniture, some exquisite lead pencil sketches framed in gray and gold, mirror back candle sconces mounted on red velvet backs and one handsome crystal chandelier made at our glassworks. A coal fire was burning in a fireplace of white marble, with a large white bear rug on the hearth. The glittering brass about the fireplace and rare Chinese and glass ornaments, with beautiful flowers about, presented a most hospitable atmosphere.

The day was beautiful. I was playing about the lawns and a little too young to understand what was going on. Much to my surprise when I looked down the long curved driveway, I saw a spanking team of horses with solid silver harness, so I was told, attached to a very smart carriage which carried a lady and gentleman of no mean rank. It was the Earl of ? and his fiancee Gladys—Countess, followed closely by a group of friends.

Well, all this pomp was merely a call by the Earl to ask my Dad, in person, if he would consider designing and making a service of glass with the name, Gladys, engraved on it and nothing more. The cost was not to be considered and there was only one condition, that the Countess must approve the set when it was completed.

After the necessary arrangements were made and the reception over, they all drove over to inspect the glass factory and to see a set of glass which was to grace the table of this distinguished family. The Countess was very much impressed and asked my father's permission to witness the making of her set, which was granted but there were so many pieces that she only saw a few made.

The entire service of glass comprised two hundred pieces in all, with the name, Gladys, engraved on each piece. The engraver was getting tired; however, the long job had inspired him to compose the following:

> "Oh, Gladys, dear, when I get through and get my pay,
> I'll dream of you by night and day.
> As I grind away upon your name

ON A VISIT TO ENGLAND, I DROVE BY THE OLD GLASSWORKS AND MADE THIS SKETCH ON A SCRAP OF PAPER 1901 THE WHITEHOUSE GLASS WORKS, THIS FACTORY WAS MANAGED BY ARTHUR J. NASH IN STOURBRIDGE ENGLAND AS A PARTNER WITH SIR EDWARD WEBB, PRIOR TO COMING TO U.S.A. TO JOIN MR. TIFFANY. IN 1892.

It makes me think of your great fame.
So love the Earl who gave you this
And seal the bargain with a kiss.

The Countess overheard these words one day and gave the man a ten pound note for a copy of them. On the day this service of glass arrived a dinner party was given, the song was sung and the engagement of the Earl and Gladys, countess of Lonsdale, was announced the following day. To please the old glass cutter she kissed the Earl.

This is a story I have heard repeated many times by my late father.

THE TIFFANY FIRE

When the Tiffany Factory was built in 1892 there was some dissatisfaction in the town of Corona, L.I., N.Y. The people were very few and only a half dozen stores made up the place. There were many meetings held and after each meeting, the next day would come a request to get out.

Father sent a man to attend these meetings and on each ocassion he reported that the leader was an unscrupulous man and did not belong. He was apart from the natives of the town. His name as I recall was Dick, a German im*m*igrant.

Dad decided to go to the people and tell them that the Factory would bring prosperity, jobs, housing, freight and many social activities. After his talk all were delighted and the Minister of the Church then asked for the blessing on this new enterprise.

Everyone was happy and smiling the next day, and some of the ladies came to call on Mother. Everything went along fine for a few months and the first part of the factory was completed and working.

One night my Mother was awakened by a bright light in her window.[69] "Fire!" she screamed and Dad and all of us were awake and gone. The factory was only two blocks across the field so *we* were soon there. My Dad had an expression on his face that I shall never forget. By that time Mother had dressed and come over to Dad. There were tears in her eyes, and as they looked, the entire front wall, forty feet high and nearly a block long crashed to the street. Dad looked at Mother and said, "Fannie, there goes my last dollar." They walked quietly home.[70]

The next day hanging on a wire across the street was a stuffed image of Dick. This was done by a secret gang called the "White Cap Gang." No one ever knew who they were but when a figure was hung in effigy, it gave a man twenty four hours to leave town or be shot. I never heard of a shooting but they say there were many.

The next morning Dad was at breakfast with the family all very sad, when the doorbell rang. It was Dick asking to see Dad. He was asked into the living room but on the way Dad caught my oldest brother's eye to follow. They were inside with the door shut.

It seems that Dick wanted money to get out of town and plenty of it. My brother was standing at the rear of Dick while Dad was looking in his desk about to write a check. My brother caught sight of Dick's hand drawing a gun from his pocket. With a swift movement he caught Dick's arm and got the gun away and hit him so hard that he went out on the floor. Dad gave me the gun and he drove to Newtown for the police.

Dick was booked for attempted murder and I was told he went to prison for many years and was never heard of from that day to this. The factory was refinanced and rebuilt and carried on for *forty* years.

I think the greatest loss Dad suffered was his life's work of steel engravings, his hobby. They were beautiful and all were destroyed along with his drawings.

THE FACTORY WHERE FAVRILE GLASS WAS MADE. CORONA, LONG ISLAND, N.Y. THIS PICTURE WAS MADE FROM A PAINTING BY THE AUTHOR JUST BEFORE THE COMPANY WAS CLOSED FOR THE LAST TIME IN 1929.

WASHINGTON RECORD

Research by Leslie C. Byer—

I quote from The Bureau of Census, Department of Commerce and Labor, Washington, D.C.—1908—Part III. "This is conspicuously the case with the glass products made in the United States dealing with art." This part of my research is of particular interest. "The discovery of glass was accidental, the facts are not known but it was used in remote times. The first glass was used for ornamental purposes such as imitation gems and beads among early remains in the Orient. Pliny is mentioned in all history of glass as the discoverer." Some doubt exists on this claim. Glass makers admit that what he discovered was a little bit off the general practice of the things that go into making glass—so called.

"The making of glass objects reached a very high degree of perfection in Egypt (I am still quoting) and in Egypt the art of using oxides, especially cobalt color was very early acquired. Until the time of Tiberius the art of glass making was largely an Egyptian monopoly. It then passed on to Spain and Britain. After the fall of the Roman Empire the manufacture of glass declined but its many uses and application soon brought about its revival. However, window glass was known to the Romans as is shown by the specimens found in Herculaneum and was not in general use until the Middle Ages."

"The application of chemistry to the industrial arts has done much to increase our knowledge of them. Old haphazard methods and selection of constituents to form the glass has now given place to exact selection made possible by knowledge obtained by scientific methods."

One more quote from the Washington record I find very interesting, "It is a far cry from Venice in the Old World to New York in the New but the Art glass of the famous artisans of Murano must now yield its prestige to the beautiful results obtained by the scientific makers of the exquisite FAVRILE glass."

FAVRILE glass gives a quality of iridescence not found in other glass. It lends charm to the observer, it fascinates and produces a feeling similar to a well-cut diamond and being hand made gives an added charm to its creation. It is an inspired thing of free form and beauty.

Even the hard-boiled buyers of merchandise got a big kick on entering our showrooms. I used to call it the Palace of Gold. In all the years I spent in the manufacture of glass I never failed to get a thrill out of this magnificent sight.

I only wish I could show you all the drawings and photographs I have preserved

TRADE MARKS (CENTER)—TIFFANY GLASS AND DECORATING CO. 1894 (LEFT)—TIFFANY STUDIOS. 1905–1930 (RIGHT)—LOUIS C. TIFFANY FURNACES. OCTOBER 1902–1929 THE TRADE MARK (CENTER), MAY BE FOUND ON LABELS OF VERY EARLY GLASS (DRAWING BY J. W. NASH)

from the first to the last piece made. The charm of FAVRILE glass was the fact that you never found a copy of it. Each piece was carefully considered from every point, proportion, color and form. Above all it must express Art form and to quote our former Secretary, Wm. H. Thomas of Yale, with many letters after his name:

"FAVRILE Glass, its beauty lies in its diversified radiance of iridescence."

Yes, our glass had charm and most people loved it. There was a warm friendly feeling about it and to drink from our wine glasses with a delicate sheared edge left nothing to be desired.

To add to the charm of FAVRILE glass it must be shown in a light which brings out its beauty of line and color, complimented by its background and on a black stand, the picture is complete.

I discovered that light reflection had much to do with the fundamental design of luster glass. It always received careful inspection so that each piece produced gave a maximum of artistic beauty.

GATHERING GLASS. FROM PAINTING
MADE 1921 BY L H NASH.

THE BLOWING OF GLASS

The position of Favrile glass in the realm of fine art is indicated by its presence in permanent collections in the leading museums of the world, and by its acceptance into positions of honor in the finest exhibitions and salons of the fine Arts.

It is interesting to note that hand-made glass work starts its form from a ball or pear shape.[71] From this, the forms are endless and to stop a worker during its blowing, gives many new and exotic forms. To watch glass blown, it is in motion at all times, its ductility, reflections and color present a picture not seen in any other type of manufacture. From a sketch on a blackboard the piece becomes fixed in form in a few minutes. I do not think that there is any other medium which can compare with glass for speed of production. This is not true of decorated glass.

The derivation of the word FAVRILE virtually means hand made. After all a trade

(TOP LEFT) A FAVRILE GLASS WORKER SHEARING GLASS PHOTOGRAPH FROM THE AUTHOR'S ALBUM. (TOP RIGHT) FAVRILE GLASS WORKERS ADD THE DECORATION. PHOTOGRAPH FROM THE AUTHOR'S ALBUM. (BOTTOM) FAVRILE GLASS WORKERS, "TAKING ON THE PONTIL." PHOTOGRAPH FROM THE AUTHOR'S ALBUM.

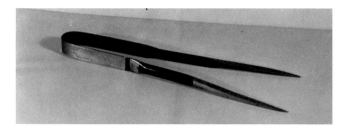

name is only intended as a means of identification. We were fortunate in having the name Tiffany associated with our product for the name in itself has been identified with quality. When you buy a diamond at Tiffany & Co. you never question its quality. All Tiffany products reflect the high order of perfection—the best that money can buy.

The vast sums of money spent to gain this perfection in some cases produced a financial loss but the high standard is foremost in the minds of all those people connected with the name. The striving for perfection in FAVRILE went on day after day, year after year. The firm made a fair profit but almost all of it went back into research and experiment.

(TOP LEFT) GLASS MAKER'S PUCELLA

(BOTTOM LEFT) GLASS MAKER'S CHAIR.
AUTHOR'S LECTURE MODELS

(RIGHT) LEHR MODEL SHOWS FINISHED
GLASS READY TO BE REMOVED FROM
THE LEHR. MOVING TRAYS CARRY THE
GLASS THROUGH THE LEHR PROVIDING
THE NECESSARY GRADUAL
TEMPERATURE REDUCTION. AUTHOR'S
LECTURE MODEL

EARLY FAVRILE GLASS
NON-LUSTER
PRIOR TO 1900[72]

These were some of the hundreds of vase forms created by my Father and for some years he refused to use his luster glass, except as a decoration in threads, but pressure was forced upon him.[73] So iridescent glass took command in full gold and blue luster. The sales were enormous.

It was at this time, 1908, that I joined the company and I remember how difficult it

FAVRILE LAMINATED GLASS FIRST PIECE OF LAMINATED GLASS MADE. AT CORONA PLANT. AUTHOR'S COLLECTION

was to keep up with orders. In *1912* I started designing all manner of things that sold like hotcakes but I was not allowed to do the sort of things that sold well. I was informed that what I was doing was too <u>commercial</u> and that I was sacrificing Art for money. It took some years before I understood what was required of me.[74]

I stopped designing anything for a time—nothing new—and the sales fell off twenty-five percent the first year and forty-five percent the second year. However, this was not all my fault. Then the Board of Directors thought I had better start designing something new of a more artistic nature. I did try very hard, but I slipped in a few of the popular items such as electric lamps, which finally wiped out the loss. America at that time was not ready for Art as understood by the few. I still say that most of the things I worked on had many elements of Art expression in line, color and form. However, as my responsibilities grew, so did my Art.

When I gave lectures on glass, many people came to me after my talk and asked questions. Most of these people think of FAVRILE glass as gold luster or blue luster. It is true that we made a large quantity of this glass. On the other hand we made just as much non-luster glass which was made more for the Art side of our business. In this glass, luster was used as a decoration and texture which, incidentially, were the pieces that won many of the honors. The fine pieces were a combination of both. Almost all the early FAVRILE glass did not use iridescent effects.

As I have already stated, both Mr. Tiffany and my Father were a little hesitant about using luster. They restricted it more to a thread or border decoration. I think Dad felt that it would overpower and tend to cheapen our other glass.

Strange to relate we had very little to do with *the* marketing *of* luster glass. The first time it appeared it was a sellout. The public just demanded it and our business grew in leaps and bounds. It was an expensive glass to make and production was slow compared with other types of glass. However, it went on its merry way and our showrooms were filled with it. To look into our showrooms on a sunny morning with this blast of iridescent color, was breathtaking. Everyone that saw this exhibition of FAVRILE glass was completely overcome and speechless at the sight. It gave one a feeling of sitting out in the tropical sun. It was literally a fairyland.

Anyone being fortunate enough to have a representative collection of FAVRILE glass should mark the price high. Tableware in plain gold luster was priced generally about two dollars or two dollars and fifty cents per inch in height, if fairly wide the price would be more. This does not apply to bowls and compotes, they were two dollars per inch in diameter, if blue luster one to two dollars additional. If carved or decorated the price could go twice as high or even more. A salt cellar at two dollars and fifty cents each was the cheapest thing we made.

IN 1921 DUE TO MANY CAUSES, THE PRICES ON ALL FAVRILE GLASS WAS INCREASED 20%, except lighting glass

Depending on its kind, size and quality, prices ranged from five dollars to five hundred dollars. Exhibition pieces have been sold from five hundred to one thousand dollars each, depending upon their importance. Peacock green vases and comports were sixty dollars and up.

Do not compare FAVRILE glass prices with anything else. Remember it will never be made again. FAVRILE glass is in a class by itself and is now occupying the same position in Art as the early painters and will become more valuable as time goes on. Many pieces have been sold for three or four times its original price. It is now difficult to find even two or three pieces of FAVRILE glass today. If you are successful you will pay a large price.

To properly identify FAVRILE glass you will see engraved on the bottom the following: on most pieces the marking will be LCT FAVRILE, Louis C. Tiffany FAVRILE or on very small pieces just FAVRILE or LCT. The numbers on pieces were used to identify prices and consigned pieces to customers. The numbers also indicate approximately the age. The numbers started with letters of the alphabet prefix as A100–A101 up to 10,000 for each letter and later the letters became affixed as 600A–601A,

EARLY FAVRILE GLASS. THERE WERE MANY INTERESTING FORMS MADE LIKE THESE BEFORE LUSTER GLASS WAS MADE IN 1900.

etc. If two letters appeared "EX" before the number, it indicated that the piece had been on exhibition and was a fine example of our glass. Most EX numbers have won prizes.

Some glass will be found without any marking. These pieces may have been stolen or removed by members of the firm but these cases are rare. On some pieces there will be found just a number like 426. This number has no meaning other than it was there as a consignment selection and it may be found many times. It refers to a design and price—used only in the office for reference.

I have not counted but there must be over one thousand pieces that I have photographed. It is difficult to believe that those forms all started with a ball of glass. It is things like this that make glass making so interesting.

When I designed a new vase, I would make a dozen or more drawings, pin them on the wall and after a round of the shops, I would go back to my drawings and invariably one of the twelve would be outstanding and fill the purpose for which it was intended.

This method of procedure was my method in almost all my designs knowing that while being made, some of the subtle detail would be lost. As I have mentioned, to be successful in making designs for glass the designer must know the technique of glass making, otherwise his designs will be a failure.

FAVRILE glass will never be made again. I am the last person left who understands the manufacture of FAVRILE glass and even if I wrote down the process no one could make it, as it has so many complications.

One curious thing is that two chemical houses will sell the same chemical by name but the reaction will be different. All the experiments were made with No. 1 but No. 2 will not give the same results. I do not understand this but I know this to be a fact. Now you can understand to some extent how difficult glass making can become.

The making of FAVRILE required close supervision in order to get the best results. This was my job for seventeen years and if I do say so, no-one could get the results in luster glass to gain the perfection which came about due to my close observation of the smallest detail.

The markings on Favrile glass pieces is a trade name and does not necessarily indicate the designer.

TO THE COLLECTOR OF FAVRILE GLASS

You will find in the early period that no luster glass was used. It's *NAME* at the factory was Laminated Glass. It's color was, black, brown and yellow, and a mixture of color brought by the reaction of one glass with the other.

These pieces of glass were original in form. The blowing appears careless, and little effort was made as to form. The important thing was the color. The treatment of this is most interesting. It had it's beginning in England when my father was making marble glass. The retarded action of the first filling in the melting pot, was done by putting the light color at the bottom of the pot and leaving it for four or five hours. The darker batch was then filled in over the color. The temperature being reduced somewhat. The light color would then slowly rise to the surface without fully combining. It was at this stage that the glass was gathered and blown.

Our Laminated glass was not understood by the public and as a result the sales were somewhat limited. It was only when small amounts of gold luster were used in combination, that our sales increased.

The Metropolitan Museum of New York City has an interesting collection of this glass. It was presented to the Museum by the late Mr. H. O. Havermeyer, a collector of Favrile glass.

Do not give much attention to the size of the piece, but look for interesting color and decoration.

Surface texture in our glass was always most important to us. certain colors require a polished surface and others required a mat effect. Luster effect always received very close attention, and in many cases was a difficult problem. However, it gave charm and originality to our glass.

SOME EARLY PIECES OF FAVRILE GLASS.
ABOUT 1912 PHOTOGRAPH TAKEN FROM
THE AUTHOR'S ALBUM

DEVITRIFICATION OF GLASS

It is known to many manufacturing glass experts, that it can ruin glass but with knowledge and experience this action can be of great value. It was used by my Father in England to produce surface texture. This texture contributed much to Favrile. The most difficult thing was heat control.

This devitrification was used by Dad only to the smallest possible extent. Controlled

THE TWO VASES OF LIGHT COLOR ARE
SEMI-CRYSTALIZED GLASS

by metal content in the batch. If devitrification is properly applied, it is possible to render glass impervious to excessive heat such as pyrex glass for cooking

Devitrification is little understood by glass makers also it is difficult to describe but it means semi-crystalized in a broad sense. It was used frequently on luster glass to gain texture effects.

There are textures on the surface of most articles. I can only describe the texture of Favrile as a surface of rare beauty as opposed to a shiny colored ball.

GLASS COMPOSITION AND HEAT CONTROL

<u>Window glass</u> including crown, cylinder and sheet glass is composed of: Silicate of Potash or soda, lime and a little alumina.

<u>Plate glass</u> is composed of: Silica, soda or potash, lime and little alumina. This glass is almost the same as above but has practically no color.

<u>Flint glass</u> is composed of: Silica potash and oxide of lead.

<u>Old Optical glass</u> also table glass is composed of: Silica or salicic acid and potash with more lead than previous glass. It is a simple flint made with the purest chemicals and iron free.

The above shows only what glass is composed of. I could go on for many pages but it would serve no purpose.

<u>FAVRILE</u> glass was a departure from glass shown above, particularly luster glass.

Temperature control was of the utmost importance and great care must be taken when weighing the materials, even to a fraction of an ounce. Even a tiny excess of iron would ruin a thousand pounds of glass. Pure clay as iron free as possible was used for melting pots but the magic was surface texture, heat control comes in again. Surface chill was carefully observed during its entire process.

Luster glass is a very complex thing to make. It took me some years to properly understand what the important things were and without my Father to teach me, I am quite sure Favrile glass could never have existed as far as I was concerned.

The purpose of mentioning a little about the composition of glass is not for the glass maker but to place in the minds of the reader how FAVRILE glass came into being.

Knowing Mr. Tiffany as I did, I am quite sure he understood my Father's position in the making of FAVRILE glass. I could tell many stories about FAVRILE and the claims that some people made, but I choose not to mention any names which could cause embarrassment.

I know the source of many statements given by persons in the employ of the two companies. Some have passed on. But you may rest assured that what I have written are from my own personal observation and knowledge of FAVRILE glass and its makers. I have my own reasons but don't let anyone fool you into believing someone else invented FAVRILE glass. All of it in basic form came from <u>Arthur J. Nash</u> and added to by my brother, <u>Douglas</u> and <u>myself</u>—<u>no one else</u>.

I have been interviewed, written to, called on the phone, questioned at my lectures and even heard that somebody said, "He wouldn't know," meaning me.

The pictures on [this] page are photographs of pieces of glass brought to America by Mr. Nash in 1892.[75] Mr. Nash was very proud of this glass because they represented an achievement long sought after. In his book of formula, it is noted as B^1 and the final formula was noted as B^2 after he made a slight change. The "B" represented "the best." This B^2 formula remain the same until the business closed. The only change ever made was by myself in the production of Peacock green luster, for which I received 25 shares of stock in the company from Mr. Tiffany and my father, as a reward.

FIRST IRIDESCENT GLASS—MADE BY ARTHUR J NASH FROM HIS NOTES, I JUDGE IT MUST HAVE BEEN ABOUT 1887 TO 1888. (NOTE TEXTURE OF GOLD ABOUT THE NECK.)

HEAT, AND FAVRILE GLASS

There are many books written about glass making in general, it's history, it's time and place, it's design and color; but, as to composition of materials, I note that many little secrets are still kept within in boundries of the family.

The time my father spent on experimental work, to perfect Luster glass in England, was well known to his family and friends. His great trouble was heat control, because at that time soft coal was used. Forced draft was tried, but only increased his troubles. In America, oil was used to gain better heat control, but there were no burners designed for this purpose. What we wanted to use, was high pressure oil and steam. After many attempts, we finally made an oil burner which worked beautifully for many years. Then, later on, we changed to low pressure air and high pressure oil. This was the best.

The burning of fuel oil was little understood at that time, and to start the furnace fire presented a problem. After blowing our furnace up, we decided to bring the heat up with wood, before turning on the oil. Whenever we did this, I always felt that I would reach heaven before my time.

I gave much time to developing perfect heat control because both father and I knew that it was important in the manufacturing of fine luster glass.

Luster glass was not expected to be a big business, but, it was demanded by the public.

It was through this heat control, that many of our finest pieces of glass came to being.

In our morning glory glass which was composed of five layers, If made in one single temperature the piece would remain clear crystal. If it were in a higher degree of heat three chemicals would combine and form one or two colors. If lower than normal, temperatures were applied, parts of the piece would become opalescent and so on. It was very much like developing a photograph—years of experiments went into this process.

It was this glass that won for us the highest award obtainable in the World of Art, a gold medal and the place of honor in the Paris salon. (See photograph) *page 81 & 82* This sensitive glass would change color if touched with the point of a nail.

Mr. Tiffany made a water color *spray* of Morning Glorys for us to work by. I could think of plenty of flowers which would not be so complicated to make in this process. We made many famous colors in vase forms, such as: Chinese red, Samian red, Mazarin blue, Royal blue, Apple green, Purple, Violet, Manderin yellow and many more.

Luster glass came in pure gold, red gold, Grotto blue, blue, blue purple, pink, blue black and *the* last my own invention of Peacock green.

You will note in many vases that the surface texture on various colors appears to have an iridescent surface. The fillings for this type of glass had to be carefully put together. Some types of glass would not respond to such treatment. For instance, needle crystal antimony unless used with restraint and care would turn out like mud. The best results were obtained when large amounts of pure gold was used. The presence of gold in glass would prevent oxidization to a point if color were introduced. Many glass makers have tried to produce luster glass but if they found the formula written down the most important chemical was always left out. Dad and I never revealed this to a living soul. If this chemical were not used the luster would in time become dull and to an extent be washed off. The strength, durability and beauty would be lost.

It was easy to tell the original of these copies. Unscrupulous people lost thousands of dollars trying to make luster glass. They didn't know and never will.

We made so many kinds of glass that I could keep on writing forever but I do not feel that I can continue unless I describe the chemical and technical side of glass making. Our glass was so complex that it would be of no value.

If I did write and give out information I should only break the trust and tradition of the glass makers that has come down through generations. Mr. Tiffany tried on many occasions to get this information in writing. I told him that I could not impart information without breaking a trust and that the knowledge I have, was given to me with that understanding. That is the way it is going to be, come what may.

EARLY FAVRILE STEM GLASS. PHOTOGRAPHIC COPY OF AN EARLY WATERCOLOR DRAWN BY MY BROTHER, PERCIVAL BREDT NASH, WHO WAS WITH US FOR ABOUT TWO YEARS.

VASE FORMS

Seldom do you find in Favrile glass vases, forms which could be termed commonplace. There is an air of refinement about them. I do not mean formal lines such as you may find among the Mid-Victorian period.

In many cases you see in our glass, forms which are original. They have the free flow of a molten mass. Forms made by us never appear tortured, they take on the contour natural to glass blowing. Many times you would feel that a design never existed, and as I

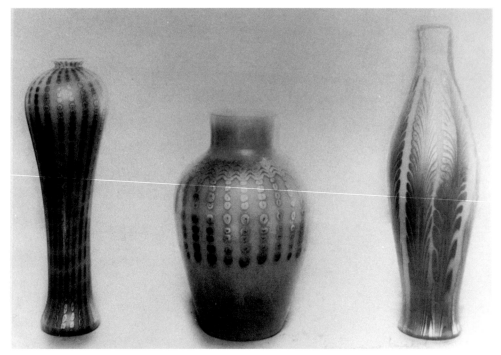

have often said, "It is impossible to design glass without a thorough knowledge of its limitations of manufacture."

Almost all designs submitted to us had to be changed to conform to the nature of the glass and its technique. If the designs do not conform, ugliness personified is the result.

I do not condemn the designers because I know it is only caused by lack of knowledge of the medium. Glass presents many problems and it is only after years of experience that you can properly become a designer of glass. A monstrosity can come about in the twinkling of the eye.

A TYPICAL MONDAY MORNING

I arrived at the factory as usual at 7:30 A.M. Dad had reached a point in his long years of work that he had no regular time of arrival. We all assembled in Dad's office. Mr. Tiffany had no office as he arrived every Monday morning at eight A.M. sharp and spent about one hour or less. Mr. Tiffany had his own big chair, Dad sat at his large desk. I sat near Mr. Tiffany because he did not hear very well. My brother sat at one end of the table with his papers and notebook. Mr. Tiffany never was without his cane and the first thing he did was to clean his glasses.

A few new pieces of glass were on Dad's desk for discussion. Fifteen minutes later after hearing my Brother read reports, etc., Mr. Tiffany headed for my studio, a kind of "do-it-yourself" place.

This studio consisted of a large drawing table, small lathe, and a work bench and the entire room was full of books, drawings, glass, enamels, lamps, flat glass samples, clocks and dozens of very interesting inventions. This Mr. Tiffany loved, but he would stay for about half-an-hour, walk through the glass house, say "Good-bye" and get into his Crain Simplex Car, and with a powerful purr of the engine, he was gone.

He would leave me completly confused because nothing had been accomplished.

THE NEW MAN

On a Monday morning a new glass worker was there in the glass house getting ready for his new job. He was employed to handle large pieces. He was a clever man but of the rough and ready type. To handle a piece 24 inches tall is a man's-sized job, it requires strength and skill and this man had it.

He was working on his first piece, I was watching him. He almost lost it but he got it into shape again. I saw Mr. Tiffany and my Father coming over to watch the new man. Mr. Tiffany did not know any of the men by name, he would just nod to them. He was dressed as usual in a pongee suit, Panama hat and carrying a cane.

The new man was having a bit more difficulty with his large vase. I looked at this man's face, a tense expression and a well chewed cigar, dripping juice down his chin, was causing him trouble, because both his hands were busy. Finally, he took the soggy driping cigar, from his mouth and handed it to Mr. Tiffany and said "Here, Bub, hold this you ain't doin nothing." Mr. Tiffany took the precious morsel and held it but disgust was written all over his face. While the new man did not know Mr. Tiffany, I doubt if he cared who*m* he gave it to.

We all had a good laugh and so did the other glass workers. All is not serious in the glass business.

THE MAGIC ROOM

This is just a brief description of our laboratory. It was on the second floor of a brick fireproof building. It was about 50 feet long and 20 feet wide. One end contained liquid chemicals with the regular laboratory equipment. The other end contained a counter on two sides and about 150 drawers used to store dry chemicals, scales, enclosed in glass, and larger scales, fume chamber, sink, first aid closet, a long pine table and two leather chairs and book case.

The door was oak with double locks and a small safe. This was the magic room where Favrile glass started its merry way into your homes and it was here where I spent

"THE MAGIC ROOM" FROM THE
PAINTING BY THE AUTHOR—1924

many lonely hours. The walls I had painted green to rest my eyes. The sunlight on the white plaster was blinding.

I was compelled to be there because if I didn't the men could not work. Often my days were long and tiring and I always wondered if the glass would be right for the next day. Double index was confusing at times but 90% of the glass was O.K. The drawers that were painted red were poison. (See painting)

Every rare chemical found its way into this room, such as: Platinum, gold, silver and diamond dust, rock crystal, rubies, emeralds, and amythists. Every chemical and metalic oxides all went through the gamut of experiment and many wonderful things came about. At the end of our business there were numerous perfected ideas which never reached the market. The glass that went into our church windows was one reason for their beautiful color effects never found in windows before or since.

I have been told that to hold back information on things which would benefit the world was a mistake. If I felt that it would benefit the world, that is one thing, but to make one man rich that is another.

There are many books on the subject of making glass so I feel that a long dissertation on the subject would be of little use. Handmade glass is becoming a thing of the past, therefore any information that I gave would be of little value to the world where commercial glass of one color is made.

The Tank furnace could not handle colored glass because it is continuous in operation. Handmade glass is melted in hooded pots. Glass of today is made under an entirely different method.

To write this information would make a very large book and few sales would result!

"NOTHING MORE FINAL"

I have often thought of my first day at the factory. When I broke the beautiful wine glasses and the remark my Father made. His remark was the inspiration for the following:

> "There is nothing more final than a piece of broke glass"
> It ceases to exist in its original mass.
> A fragment held all wet with tears,
> Lives only in memory down through the years."

LHN

A LOVER OF GLASS

Expectancy of form,
Ductility of mass,
Color sublime,
A tinkle, thats glass

L H N

Certain kinds of glass while being ground on the bottom and when a smoothing wheel is used, *sometimes* creates a bell-like sound. If you stand close to the worker during this sound and sing the same note the glass will shatter. The thickness and kind of glass has much to do with this.

Let us praise, admire and exhault the glassmakers down through the centuries. Those who have worked ceaselessly to contribute more to better living and service, than almost anyone I can think of. Count all the windows in New York City alone. What could be used to give light and keep out the cold which would last for a hundred years or more.

Glass is truly a wonderful creation. I ask you to look about you and it will be a surprise to see how much glass enters into your life. Try to think what it would be like without any.

Here is a start, no Television, no light, no tableglass, no containers, no windows, no bottles, and no mirrors. What would the ladies do then—poor things.

I'll leave the list for you to finish and you will discover that it is almost endless on the commercial side only.

Now we turn to Art

As expressed in Glass and here you will discover how beautiful glass can be in church windows, mosaics, everything in places of worship through the centuries, vases, plates, bowls, candlesticks, loving cups. I could go on almost forever, but I don't need to convince anyone of the great value of glass.

Mr. Tiffany and Father were always a great source of inspiration to me.

WHAT GLASS MEANS TO ME

A Condensed Story of Favrile Glass

When I was about High School age, a piece of glass to me was a water pitcher, ashtray, tumbler, a pressed or moulded vase for flowers, a window pane, a milk bottle or a butter dish. Little did I think at that time, that I was destined to become a member of a firm of famous glass manufacturers.

After a touch of the bends received under the East River during the building of the Pennsylvania Railroad Tunnel, I decided that engineering was not for me. After my recovery, in the latter part of 1908, I became associated with the Tiffany Furnaces, Inc. at Mr. Tiffany's request. The company was founded by my father, the late Arthur J. Nash and the late Louis C. Tiffany. During my time the Board of Directors consisted of Louis C. Tiffany—President, Arthur J. Nash—Vice-President, A. Douglas Nash—Secretary and Treasurer, Charles L. Tiffany, George F. *Heydt*, Wm. H. Thomas and myself.[76]

My job was designer and general supervisor of the factory production which had many departments but for many years the glass house was my important work. As my father advanced in years, I took over more and more of his work in the Laboratory which required constant study. The chemistry I had learned in school was of little use in the glass business. I had studied designing and painting in England, France and America which was a tremendous help to me in a business dedicated to Art.

As my responsibility grew and before taking on designing in glass, I decided to look over the glass that had been made in Ancient Egypt and follow its path to America. There are many books on the subject and they deal almost entirely with dates and places. This was not exactly what I wanted, because the writers in most cases did not understand just what glass was made of or how it was made. The artistic side was neglected and it was this long research that inspired me later to lecture on glass and its manufacture.

GLASS BLOWING WITH A CAPITAL "B"

There were times when the glass pots had an excess of glass left over and usually they were ladled out into large caldrons containing water which cracked up the glass into small lumps. This was called "moil" and was used again with fresh chemicals.

Every now and then the men asked if they might use up some of the glass on their own time. I never refused because it was difficult to use up the extra glass. The men each put up $1.00, appointed three judges and the man that could blow the largest ball perfectly round, if possible, won the prize money. As I remember, there was even a second prize.

The sight of this contest was really something to see. Everyone tried, men and boys, and even the men who attended the fires. The glass was all colors and the reflections were just beyond description. The balls would blow sideways, pointed, two at a time, or just pop out on one side. Some of the more experienced men blew balls up to 20 inches in diameter. After that size they could not get the ball into the furnace for reheating.

This was exciting to see. I have never seen so much glass in action. It was wonderful.

THE GLASS BLOWERS PARADE

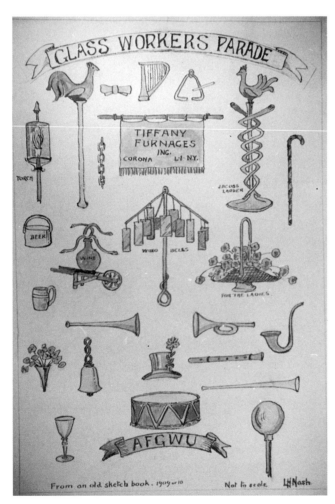

In the early days of my Father's experiences in glass manufacturing in Stourbridge, England, Dad told a story about the holiday for glass workers called the Blowers Parade or Walking Day. I rather doubt if there is a person living today who witnessed the Parade he told about. This Parade was duplicated in Corona, Long Island, New York where our factory was located and if I remember correctly it took place about one year after I became associated with the firm, about 1909.

To put this show on involved a tremendous amount of work for those taking part. Permission was granted to the men to use the glass necessary for making gadgets for the parade. I can't remember all the things but here is a partial list: glass hats of every shape, walking sticks, glass badges were struck from the press, pipes, lanterns, musical instruments, such as: long trumpets, triangles, drums, bells of all kinds and sizes, baskets of flowers for the ladies, flip flops, Jacob ladders, colored balls, glass chains for necklaces, wind bells on tall rods, mugs for beer and a lot more. About one hundred men took part and were followed by the men working in other departments. Of course, a brass band, banners and colorful costumes and the United States Flag. I tell you this was a ball. They all gathered at the little Pond where kegs of beer and food of all kinds was enjoyed by all. People came from far and wide and in the evening they had a torch light Parade. From what I saw there was very little of the delicate glass objects left. I have often thought what fun it would be to own this collection of beautifully made things. When the sun shone on them the colors and crystal pieces were a sight to behold. To my knowledge it was never repeated. The time and material were a little more than the Company cared to spend. The man who put the show on was old John Hollingsworth, head of our wine glass shop. He was the only one who could remember the Parade in England. He was one of our oldest workers and worked for Dad in England.

VENETIAN GLASS

Venetian glass remained a mystery for many years. Those of you who have some early Venetian glass have noted the flaked gold effect. This was known as fools gold or avonturine. It was a fact that many glassmakers tried to make it but they all failed; some thought it was real gold.

This was not the case. This crystalline effect is brought about by a copper reaction. The entire pot of glass is withdrawn from the furnace and allowed to cool very slowly in a kiln. The glass crystalizes and when remelted or drawn in canes the effect remains. Dad made many experiments, the difference being instead of gold, Dad was trying for a green crystalline effect which he accomplished. The piece I have is conclusive proof. We never put any on the market as it was just an experiment.

This avonturine crystal was threaded on to clear glass, twisted, drawn into cane and broken into short lengths then arranged in circular form on end. Fresh glass is forced into the rods which adhere to the clear glass. It is all reheated, melted together and blown into various objects. Plain colors are also used.

The early Venetian glass workers were remarkable, in fact, they were the best I have ever seen.

SOAPSTONE MOLDS

Just a note. I was told by Mr. Barber of the Philadelphia Museum that some of the early bottles were blown into soap stone molds. This was the first time I had heard of them. About two months later he sent me one. It was broken but I wired it together and blew glass into it. The heat did not affect it in the least. Never too old to learn. Soapstone permits the carving of designs. I suppose iron molds were hard to get and expensive in the early days.

COLORED GLASS BALLS

Every now and then a dealer in downtown New York City would order 100 red glass balls, 100 white glass balls and 100 green glass balls. I often wondered what they were for.

After a visit to Cape Cod some years later, I discovered that they were put into net bags and tied to the fishermens nets and the colors identified the owner of the nets.

There were so many strange things ordered from us, but I think almost anyone could have explained those glass balls if questioned.

GOLD RUBY

It is interesting to tell how varying temperatures can change the density of certain kinds of glass. Ruby glass had its origin in Germany and it contained pure gold. When this glass is melted, taken from the pot and blown, it is almost clear, with very little color showing, but when cooled the color starts to develop. When reheated and cooled again, the color increases more and the true ruby color appears. This can be repeated until the color is so dense you would think it is black. Many beautiful effects can be produced by this treatment.[77]

A wine glass can be made by partly heating the bottom of the bowl causing a shading from dark to pale ruby at the top. While working with Ruby glass, I tried touching it in parts with a cold steel knife or file and I discovered that almost any desired pattern could be effected.

This method I advanced to a point which was the beginning of the Famous Morning Glory glass. Dad understood what I was trying and suggested some changes in the formula, which made the glass more sensitive. Out of this glass came our highest award. Many effects had their origin in this manner.

CUT GLASS

Hardly a week passes that I am not asked about cut glass. In the early days of our glass making we made cut glass but unlike the regular type, we used crystal with a tint of color. This was very brilliant, jewel like in effect but we discontinued it because everyone was trying to copy it. From what I saw it became a common thing and badly done.

If people could only know that they spend more money trying to copy others than they would if they created something of their own! It is bad business because it cheapens the product so much that no one profits by copying and all that they have accomplished is to destroy the market for the original product. This was the case in cut glass, every one wanted to get into the act.

Quality crystal for cutting makes a lot of difference to the brilliance of the cutting. That is the reason you find so much off color cut glass. To make cut glass requires an expert to do the cutting and an expert to make the glass.

The society of cutters was a business all its own and they purchased blanks from glass manufacturers. There were only two or three that made their own glass in this country. Much was imported from England and France.

Really fine cut glass is hard to find and great care must be exercised when making a selection. There are books on the subject.

(TOP) CAMEO FLASK COLOR IS RUBY AND YELLOW, CARVED IN DEEP RELIEF.

(BOTTOM) CAMEO GLASS

CAMEO GLASS

This is produced by carving or grinding through one color to another. Some call it engraving.

Some wonderful things have been made by the use of this method of decoration. It is not easy and takes years of practice to make a worthy looking example. Etching has been tried but it never can equal engraved glass.

The man doing this must be an Artist to some extent and a good draftsman with a steady hand. One slip and out it goes.

Many engravers on glass originated in Germany. You seldom find young men doing this kind of work. I think they become discouraged at the length of time required to gain perfection. Also to sit in one position for eight hours is more than they can endure.

We made many pieces of Cameo glass and they were very expensive due to the long hours spent on them.

An outside green cut to expose yellow was a favorite with us. The cost was $100.00 and up. Our engraving shop consisted of five men and all were experts at their trade. You may be able to find a piece but it will be very expensive.

Many of our Cameo Lampshades were made after this method.

ROCK CRYSTAL

The [photo below] is a Rock Crystal vase 18^1/$_2$ inches tall, heavily carved. This vase is a creation of my Father, Arthur J. Nash. It was made from his formula for Rock Crystal. There is no mold used. The glass is pure Rock Crystal. The design and decoration was entirely his own. The vase was thick and the floral design was engraved deep by the best man in the trade *whose* time card showed 181 hours.

My father was very proud of this glass. The charm of this glass was its delicate Florescence which gave an effect somewhat like moonstone only more delicate. It is difficult to describe but it was exquisite. He made about four or five of these vases and the price was well over five hundred dollars each. This cost is due to many hours of cutting and engraving required for the deep relief.

I am sorry that I do not possess one of these beautiful vases. It was his last creative effort. My father's fine mind is expressed so magnificently in this exquisite form and decoration with a moonstone quality in the glass. No words can do justice to this piece when placed in a proper light.

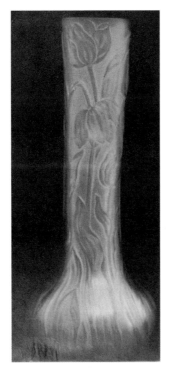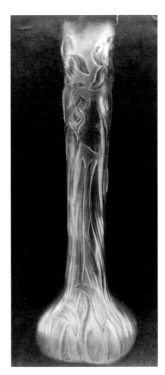

A BEAUTIFUL EXAMPLE OF ENGRAVED ROCK CRYSTAL BY ARTHUR J NASH A PRIZE WINNING PIECE 23 INCHES TALL PRICE—$875.00 PHOTOGRAPHED FROM FADED PICTURE IN AUTHOR'S ALBUM.

CANDLESTICKS

There are great numbers of glass candlesticks but most of them are crystal—plain, pressed, handmade and cut. Some have hurricane globes, tall chimney form swelled in the middle and there are the inverted bell shapes. Many will have cut drops hanging. There are single, double, three, four, and five candles used. They make a very interesting item to collect but are rather expensive. You will find a great variety. I have seen some in color.

From the Sandwich Co. at Cape Cod there were dolphins with blue base and white top.[78] From what Dad told me the mould was originally used in his factory in England. He sold many obsolete moulds to the Sandwich Co. through Mr. Phesingdon who came to England to purchase moulds which had been discontinued.

PAPERWEIGHTS

Paperweights are very old and I have been unable to establish their origin but almost every handmade glass factory or small single pot-home type furnace has at sometime produced glass paperweights.

The men in our factory would make them during lunch hour. Some were very poor but on the other hand some were very beautiful. Floral effects were rather difficult and required a glass maker with experience and a knowledge of Art to say nothing of the many colors required. I have seen wonderful ones made in China and also in England. I am told some were made in France but the lack of marking makes them rather difficult to identify. The main feature of a paperweight is to eliminate the bubbles—that is the difficult thing to do.

On the other hand, the bubbles are formed purposely into a design, graduated from large to small. These are done with the aid of a mould, then covered with moulton glass by dipping it into the pot which imprisons the bubbles. Some paperweights are very brilliant when made after this method.

These paperweights make a wonderful thing to collect and express the glass workers skill to perfection. Select them with care.

COIN GLASS

A wine glass with a hollow stem containing a gold coin was presented to my Father while on a visit to London. The gentleman lived in London and at the death of his Father inherited a large fortune, but a firm of lawyers managed to get almost all of it.

His mother lived in America and *had known* my Father *for many* years. She asked Father if he would meet her son in London and added that you will know him when he presents you with a Wine glass containing a gold coin, which you made for my husband in England thirty years ago.

After meeting my son will you question him about his estate, something has gone wrong. After meeting the Gentleman and hearing his story, Father put some lawyers to work on the case and recovered almost all of the estate.

Dad was happy with his glass, it lay about our house for years. One day a careless maid broke it while dusting. Dad had the coin on his watch chain for many years and enjoyed telling the story about it.

I may add that it takes an expert glassworker to do this trick.

COIN GLASS

GLASS DECORATION

Now let us talk a little about glass decoration. Decoration on glass is as old as time itself. The Egyptians introduced very thin rings of colored glass applied while the glass was hot and fused into the body of the piece.

The many ways to decorate a piece of glass is endless. The most common effects are produced by moulding and blowing, pressing designs, laid on and tooled, sand blasting, etching, cutting, carving, engraving, enameling and other. Surface texture was important to us.

Much of our decoration, new to the Glass world, was chemical reactive glass which I will explain later on.

LUSTER FOUND ON ANCIENT GLASS

The decomposition of early glass found in Egypt, Cyprus and many other places.

Pottery of the Han dynasty and Persian pieces, in fact much of the glass has this iridescence but it was not made that way. The glass was common and many pieces show a green tinge.

The iridescence is caused first by the length of time under ground and is the result of carbon dioxide or Atmospheric Carbonic acid which dissolves parts of the alkali and liberates the silica.

This action can be seen at the Metropolitan Museum. Ask for Han pottery also Cypriote glass.[79] It is very beautiful. Also, while there, see some interesting pieces of

FAVRILE GLASS COPIES OF "CYPRIOTE"
GLASS. NOTE SURFACE TEXTURE.
AUTHOR'S COLLECTION

Favrile glass. Many of the pieces were made during the early period of our glass, prior to the use of luster glass.

These pieces of the <u>early</u> glass were presented by Mr. H. O. Havermeyer, an ardent collector of our early glass. There is also a Tiffany Favrile glass window on the stairway going down to the lower floor.

Copies of this ancient glass were made by me personally and only very few pieces were made. I am not a glass worker but I personally made them. The crater-like texture was very difficult to make.

EARLY EGYPTIAN GLASS INSPIRES POEM THESE EARLY PIECES OF EGYPTIAN GLASS WERE THE INSPIRATION FOR MY POEM "A GLASS THREAD FIVE THOUSAND YEARS LONG."

SOME EUROPEAN FORMS OF GLASS DECORATION

FIGURE 4. EARLY EGYPTIAN GLASS, XVIII–XX DYNASTIES

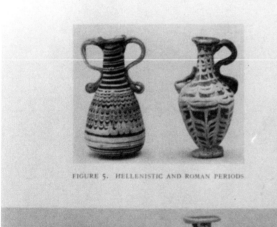

FIGURE 5. HELLENISTIC AND ROMAN PERIODS

Sprinkled fragments of various colors were put on a Marver or Iron table and just before blowing the pieces are picked up by rolling the hot glass over the broken glass, reheated and blown into the final form.[80]

To cover a piece of glass there are many ways, such as: cupping, covering and flashing.

<u>Cupping</u> is like dropping moulten glass into a cup made of hot glass and then blown.

<u>Covering</u> is taking glass from one pot and dipping it into another of a different color.

<u>Flashing</u> is a method of producing a shaded color from dark to light. It is accomplished by dipping the blow iron into a color—picking up a bit of glass about as big as a button and then the blow iron takes on the required amount of *clear* glass. When blown the color fades out, if blown very large it would fade out completely.

There are hundreds of ways to decorate the surface of glass and it is interesting to try to discover how it was done.

<u>Threading</u>—You will notice that I speak of threading. This is accomplished by winding hot threads of glass about the piece before expanding it. This is also accomplished in later years by turning the blow pipe in a machine and creating an evenly spaced thread. Then

while the object is very hot, the *th*reads are pulled with a hook, up and down, making a design. The piece is then blown and tooled into it's final form.

Notice carefully how this was accomplished in Ancient glass and also on Favrile glass. It is the oldest method of decoration known to the glass trade and requires skill to produce worthy results.

A GLASS THREAD

5000 THOUSAND YEARS LONG
BY LESLIE HAYDEN NASH

Kindled in the furnace glow,
A fire burned incandescent, slow,
Melting down ash bone and sand,
Making Glass for all the land.

Then dipping into the molten mass
A thread is born by stretching glass
This thread runs back five thousand years,
To decorate bottles for mourners tears.

This delicate thread has woven its way,
Down through the years to the present day,
It has graced the cups of Vikings bold,
And enhanced the beauty of the Venetian
    bowl.

In Cypress Isle, where glass was found
Buried in tombs beneath the ground,
Its lusterous beauty with patches of white,
Revealed a thread of gold so bright.

This glass is now in museums care,
Unknown by all, that a thread is there,

To the Glass man and Collectors, tho,
The thread to them is half the show.

There are leaves and stems and little dots
Damescene borders and Forget-me-nots,
Delicate threads on decanters rare
A warning to tipsters, who may come there

The little glass ships that pass in the night
With sails of thread, what a brilliant sight,
And Oh, so many other things,
All made so pretty of tiny glass strings.

It stretched across the sea they say
To America, where its used today,
On Favrile glass it was spun in gold
Now the story of the thread is told.

Fear not my friends and shed no tears
It has lasted now five thousand years,
Someone will pick up this valued thread,
And use it again,————It is not dead.

FAVRILE TABLE GLASS

The following were carried as open stock patterns: Quart and Pint decanters, liqueur, sherry, claret, champagne, whiskey and soda, old-fashioned, water goblet, fingerbowl, ice plate, compotes, pitchers, cake plates, salts and peppers, flower vases, candlesticks, BonBon and others. It would really be something to use all at a dinner party and would cost a fortune. We have sent out many times, services of over four hundred pieces. Many sets were of special design with monograms, crests, coats-of-arms, etc.

As a gift for the Royal family of Japan we made a set of Lotus Blossom design, deeply engraved, representing the open flower.[81] It was hand carved and lined with delicate gold and blue luster, one of the most beautiful sets that ever left our factory. The champagne glasses cost fifty dollars each. Other pieces were priced in proportion.

(TOP LEFT) THE SPORTMANS FAVORITE THIS SET INSPIRED BY THE EARLY BOTTLE CALLED
THE "LEATHER BOTTELLE", WAS DESIGNED BY ARTHUR J. NASH. THE GLASSES WERE
MADE TO MATCH, AND THE TRAY WAS OF HAND HAMMERED COPPER, USING THE
HONESTY LEAF OR MONEY PLANT AS DESIGN MOTIF. FACTORY PRICE—GLASS $125.00
TRAY $100.00 AUTHOR'S COLLECTION

(TOP RIGHT) FAVRILE GLASS DECANTER AND GLASSES.

(MIDDLE LEFT) FAVRILE TABLE GLASS FROM THE AUTHOR'S COLLECTION.

(MIDDLE RIGHT) SPECIAL FAVRILE TABLEWARE THREE TALL GOBLETS—COLORS, RUBY
AND OPAL WITH GREEN STEMS TWO CEREMONIAL WINES, COLOR PALE GREEN WITH
BLOWN STEMS. AUTHOR'S COLLECTION 1957

(BOTTOM LEFT) FAVRILE GOLD LUSTER TABLEWARE AUTHOR'S COLLECTION

When I look at pressed and moulded pieces of glass that people collect today, of
which many are beautiful in their own way, I find it very difficult to appreciate some of
this glass from a glass makers point of view. There is one exception—Lalique, the highest

(TOP LEFT) FAVRILE GOLD LUSTER TABLEWARE "PRINCE" 1-SHERRY 2-CLARET 3-CHAMPAGNE 4-GOBLET AUTHOR'S COLLECTION

(TOP RIGHT) FAVRILE GOLD LUSTER TABLEWARE AUTHOR'S COLLECTION

(BOTTOM LEFT) FAVRILE GOLD LUSTER TABLEWARE AUTHOR'S COLLECTION

(MIDDLE RIGHT) FAVRILE GOLD LUSTER PUNCH BOWL. FOURTEEN INCH DIAMETER—DAMASCENED—LIST $500.00 AUTHOR'S COLLECTION

(BOTTOM RIGHT) FAVRILE TABLE GLASS

expression of Art in moulded glass. I like to see the hand of the craftsman and the surface texture brilliant with fire polish. My mind always goes back and sees the dexterity of handling, blowing and shearing. The golden light on the mens' faces from the gloryholes, this is glass making to me. It is a strange thing that the commonplace sets in, when those in quest for money lay aside the great expression achieved by the creative arts.

There are so many exquisite pieces of glass listed in books and catalogues, with pieces on display in Museums. Most manufacturers are quite familiar with the early glass. But this is not my story, I only use the antique to demonstrate a point. It is all so interesting that I find it difficult to stay with my subject—FAVRILE glass.

If our table glass could be considered commercial, glass which many times out class other products considered as art, then this is a liberal interpretation of the word 'commercial.' Two or three dozen pieces of one design is hardly commercial, and as far as I am concerned, Art <u>was</u> expressed in all of our glass.

I have been interviewed many times on this subject. I always ask the same question—"Do you know what Art is?" If the answer is "No" my answer is "No comment." I really do not know how the word commercial became a point of comment. Mr. Tiffany hated interviews and seldom gave one. If anyone knew Mr. Tiffany better than I did, I can say that many of the remarks attributed to him never came from him. I do know that some persons, to hold their jobs, would give out statements in his name simply to flatter him.

I have reason to believe that many who have written about FAVRILE glass have little experience in the appearance of Art. I have been teaching Art appreciation and painting for over twenty five years and I do not have to tolerate the many inaccurate remarks about Mr. Tiffany or anyone else in our company. I have a great many clippings on this subject and few of them have told the truth throughout. This probably came about because very few interviews were granted and no one was permitted in our factory. Therefore, what they did not know, they made up.

I attended a lecture on FAVRILE glass and the gentleman that was speaking told us that he worked at the Tiffany Glass Works and produced many of the things for Mr. Tiffany. I sat there amazed, I just could not believe my ears.

After the lecture I was standing talking to a friend when a lady brought the gentleman up to introduce him and said, "I think you will have much in common." I asked him how he had the nerve to say what he did and to prove his claim. He turned red in the face and walked out without saying a word to anyone.

AQUAMARINE GLASS

A further developement in our glass came about when Aquamarine glass made it's appearance.[82] I had many disappointments in trying to make this glass, and the

AQUAMARINE GLASS FISH AND SEAWEED DESIGN IN SOLID GLASS. THIS PIECE CRACKED DURING IT'S MANUFACTURE. FROM THE AUTHORS COLLECTION

FAVRILE "AQUAMARINE" GLASS WATER LILIES PHOTOGRAPH TAKEN FROM THE AUTHOR'S ALBUM

experiments lasted much longer than I had anticipated. My main trouble being one of distortion. It came about due to the design of the form.

There is room for discussion about some of these pieces, with regards to form. Even so, every phase of it's developement was gone over carefully.

There were two kinds of Aquamarine glass. One in which water lilies appeared. The second, in which fish, nets and seaweed appeared. Both kinds were made from solid glass, except for the top, which had a depression about two or three inches deep, to give the effect of a vase filled with water. The main color of this solid glass piece, was green. We tried to obtain the same shade of gray-green and seagreen, found in the famous chinese "Celadon" porcelain. Other colors were added to form fish, stems, lilies, and nets etc.

Very few pieces of this type of glass were made, although one beautiful waterlily piece was Exhibited in Paris, and won the award. The price of each piece, at that time was about two hundred to two hundred and fifty dollars.

All pieces were interesting and colorful to look at, but difficult and expensive to make.[83]

POT SETTING—THE DREADED CALL

Many of the things I have told about have an artistic or romantic atmosphere, but there are some things the glassworker has to contend with, which are not so pleasant.

This job has been done for hundreds of years and strange as it may seem, the methods have never been improved. I am speaking of removing a cracked or broken melting pot and replacing it with a new one in a furnace where our type of glass was made.

Glass melting furnaces can be almost any size and almost any shape. Our large furnace was about twenty-three feet in diameter, with a chimney reaching up eighty to one hundred feet tall, starting the same size as the furnace and about ten feet in diameter at the top. The furnace contained sixteen pots placed in circular form in arches and built

DESIGN NAMES

up with bricks at the front of the pot, sealing them all in, with only the mouth showing. The pots can be any capacity from a monkey pot holding about fifty pounds of glass set four in an arch to the largest size used in our plant. The pots have a thick wall and are of the hooded type, oval at the base and a dome top, the only opening extends a little out through the breastwall where they are filled with the raw material, melted at 2000°, with oil and air as fuel.

After a month or so these pots become pitted at the base and finally leak glass which gets under *the* pot. This glass becomes like thick molasses and makes the task of removing it very difficult. The delay in getting it out after the breastwall is down causes the furnace to lose heat rapidly and if it is not carried out promptly the other pots may crack.

On a late November morning I entered the glass house. There was an air of hustle about, we were trying to finish up some orders for Christmas.

The thing I was most interested in was a set of table glass for one of Japan's Royal family. The Lotus design made of fluorescent glass, carved deeply, expressing the Lotus Flower, with a delicate gold luster, was without doubt the most beautiful set of glass ever to leave the factory.

I was watching the careful shearing of the lip on a champagne glass, when all of a sudden my eye caught a bright spot directly in front of *the* glass *pot* in the furnace being used for the Lotus set. The glass in this pot was difficult to make and might cause trouble in matching the exact color if anything happened to it, there would be a delay.

My heart sank as I watched the leak get larger, I called the forman, he examined it and said, "Boss, she's gone and leaking fast." I had him ladle out the glass to save what I could and told him to get ready to replace the pot with a new one and to inform the men. He left me and walked about the glass house calling, "Pot setting tonight, Pot setting tonight at seven." On hearing this call every man in the plant, whether glass worker or not had to answer it.

It had been snowing hard all day, transportation had come to a standstill. At four thirty some of the men tried to get to their homes but only those living close by could make it.

I sent out for some food and about 5:30 the glasshouse was filled with the smell of coffee, and steak and onions cooking. A golden light from the furnaces fell on a brick here, a bit of iron there, setting everything with jewels. Some of our old workmen sitting about in the soft yellow light made a perfect Rembrandt. Things looked peaceful but underlying the men's faces was a grim look, knowing, that behind the breastwall of the furnace was seething heat of 2000° which would scorch and blister their naked bodies. Some of our men were prize fighters. They have told me many times that they would rather go into a ten-round fight with a knockout than face that open arch of the furnace.

Gradually the equipment was brought in, eighteen foot crowbars, wheeled bar rests or pigs as they were called, piles of fire brick, clay, straw, long devil pitchforks for building brick work, the huge pot carriage and many other implements. Checking up, the foreman reported to me that fifty men and boys answered the call and that he had seven shifts of

THE GLASS MELTING FURNACE MODELS USED FOR AUTHOR'S GLASS LECTURES, SHOW GENERAL CONSTRUCTION OF OUTSIDE AND INSIDE OF GLASS FURNACE. NOTE THE GLASS POTS.

men to work in relays of three or less minute shifts. This meant that every man worked and then rested twenty minutes.

It was now time to remove the old cracked melting pot from the furnace and replace it with a new one. Each group took their positions and the foreman of the pot setting, took his place to give directions to the men who worked with crow bars breaking down the walls around the cracked pot, exposing them to an intense heat, each blow taking away a few bricks, each time the heat becoming more intense. Then came the order to rake away the hot bricks. The interior of the twenty three foot furnace was now quite visible. The high pressure oil burners hissing and struggling to maintain the temperature, now dropping rapidly while the arch was open. The foreman called, "Prize her loose" this was done with three short bars at close range and was the most difficult of all because the melted glass had congealed and chilled under the pot which made it fast to the floor or "siege" of the furnace. The moment was intense, the men stripped to the waist worked hard, their sweating bodies blistered by the intense heat and frequently falling chips of white hot brick.

I could not stand any closer than twenty feet from the open furnace but the men who used the short bars were only four feet away. This had to be done in order to slide the pot carriage under the pot which was then pulled out. A most difficult thing to do. The old pot was then moved away and the new one wheeled out of the oven or pot arch where it had been heating to almost furnace heat. It was then rolled into the furnace and bricked up, laid with open joints. When completed, balls of clay mixed with straw called "plastoons" were thrown with force at the wall, then an outer wall was built up with fire clay, whitewashed and the job was finished.

The men exhausted, lie about in blankets and heavy coats slowly cooling off while the dear old factory man with the whiskers cleans up the debris, whistling as though nothing happened. But the pot was set, the glass was saved and the floor of the furnace and pots on each side of the arch had been preserved. Perhaps, he did have something to whistle about.

FAVRILE GLASS AT ITS BEST

FAVRILE glass has a rich beauty all its own. With its form and rich colors, gold, blue and green lusters, you never get tired of it and it is difficult to give it a period.

In churches it gives one a warm reverent feeling. Like all Favrile products, no matter for what use, you can always depend upon quality, and with few exceptions, an excellent rendition of Artistic values.

Favrile glass if only a single piece can lend charm to any room if properly placed and lighted. Had you been fortunate enough to have walked through our showrooms, you could not come away without a feeling of having been transported into another world of great richness.

Small things lying about were like jewels of rare beauty relieved by a bright spot of red or the glow of a golden light from table lamps.

To pass cigarettes from a Favrile enamel bronze box gives prestige and makes you a host of distinction. Nothing can add to the charm when drinking wine from a delicate stem glass. To adorn your table with goblets of shades of red, green stem and foot, makes Christmas a delight. Comportiers, tall epergnes and bowls of fruit, with candlesticks present a romantic atmosphere.

If the vase is looked at with the eye of an artist, he does not see the commonplace, he looks upon it as something creative. Not only its form and decoration but he observes how well the color has been handled—and then again a marvelous quality brought about by its texture. To look over our stock, I doubt very much if you could find a color missing.

The prices of vase forms was judged entirely by its Artistic appearance, quality and size. Special Exhibition pieces ran as high as one thousand dollars each.

To describe all the glass we made would be an endless task but through these few lines, I have tried to show how Art was expressed in Favrile glass.

MORNING GLORY
CHEMICAL REACTIVE GLASS

In all my experience in glass making, I don't think I ever found anything to compare with reactive glass. It is still a mystery, to a large extent, how it comes about. I know how to do it but I don't know why so many effects can develop.

I will try to explain in part how this remarkable glass is produced. Unfortunately I cannot give the composition of the various glasses used to obtain the effects produced.

First of all hundreds of experiments were tried to gain the desired colors. They have come close but I doubt if actual perfection will ever be made.

The vase which gave us the highest award ever given for glass was called Morning Glory glass. The award came from the Paris Salon. This glass was given the place of honor at the head of the grand staircase in a special cabinet and on the walls forming a kind of background were hung the winning painters. (See photographs of Salon and glass.)

I will try to explain this new invention, never to my knowledge has this method ever been done before. First of all there are five kinds of glass and in appearance all clear flint. Each of these glasses had to be very carefully made. The contents were weighed to a fraction of an ounce. Purity of materials was essential to success. A fraction one way or another would upset the entire process. In each case a new melting pot had to be used, carefully glazed with the same batch which is used in the glass to be produced.

Now all five glasses were filled into *SEPARATE* pots and *later* blown proofs were taken after about 48 hours, furnace temperature running at 2110°F the proofs were perfect.

Now to test the reaction a ball of glass was gathered on the blowpipe—then two or three rings of another glass applied to the first. This was then blown into a ball about six inches in diameter. This ball was cooled to less than 1500° and put into a special glory-hole with a high temperature of 2340° thermo reading—kept in this heat for about 10 minutes *or less*, withdrawn, cooled and heated once more and then cooled. The most beautiful prismatic colors appeared.

PARIS SALON 1921 MORNING GLORY GLASS RECEIVES PLACE OF HONOR. HIGHEST AWARD EVER GIVEN TO ART GLASS.

This effect was too strong, now a third glass was introduced as a kind of neutralizer. This was then plunged into a temperature somewhat higher. The color after cooling was softer and more sensitive to change. So much so, that to touch it with a razor blade would produce a new color, even a pinpoint would react.

This condition was now receptive to the slightest change. Cold "pr*u*nts" were lightly touched to the surface. Somewhat like the cutter to make heart-shaped biscuits. This was then covered with the fourth glass and heated and flower "pr*u*nts" were impressed lightly and all was finally covered with the remaining glass. The entire piece was then cooled to a little over 1000° and finally plunged once more into about 2350° remaining long enough for the heat to impregnate the entire mass.

It was then removed and the colors were not quite the same as expected but I felt that slight adjustments could be made to give a little more definition to the decoration. The result was mysterious and offered many new effects still to be made.

To describe this interesting experiment is difficult but it is very much like developing a photograph, first nothing, then the picture.

(TOP LEFT) PRIZE WINNING GLASS AND
4" × 4" LUSTER TITLES. WATER COLOR OF
MORNING GLORIES BY L. C. TIFFANY.
TILES 4" × 4" GOLD LUSTER, $1.50 EA.
TILES 4" × 4" "BLUE [LUSTER] 2.00 [EA.]
DECORATED TILES ARE TAKEN FROM
CHINESE SWORD GUARDS.

(TOP RIGHT) REACTIVE GLASS WON
MANY AWARDS—3 GOLD MEDALS VERY
MUCH ADMIRED. ABOUT 14" TALL PRICE $

(BOTTOM RIGHT) CHEMICAL REACTIVE
GLASS, FROM PAINTING BY THE AUTHOR
ITEM 3# I (LEFT), AND ITEM #2, (CENTER)
ARE MORNING GLORY GLASS.

Mr. Tiffany became very much interested and one morning he brought a watercolor painting of a spray of Morning Glories, and smiling as he went out, said, "Try these with your new glass". We did, and with fair results.

These experiments cost about $12,000.00, and about twelve pieces were finally made. The price was $1000.00 each.

I cannot claim full invention of this glass, because, I received advice from both my father and brother Douglas. They told me that I was trying to do the impossible.

It was named "Morning Glory Glass". I may say, that no flower that I can think of, could offer a more difficult problem.

Under a watchful eye the high standard of Favrile products is maintained. The clever craftsmanship and intelligence of our men cannot be matched.

"MAZARIN" FAVRILE GLASS"

"MAZARIN" FAVRILE GLASS"

This celebrated blue has been reproduced in the glazes of several of the famous porcelain makers of various periods, but until the present time it has not found so satisfactory an art expression in glass. The depth of translucency and purity of color exhibited in this type of Favrile glass probably could not be excelled by any porcelain production, for the reason that the color on porcelain is a thin layer of glaze (or glass) while in the present product the entire substance is a body of glass reflecting light, and thereby giving great depth of color.

(FAR LEFT) SPRAY OF MORNING GLORIES THIS WATERCOLOR SKETCH BY MR. TIFFANY WAS THE INSPIRATION FOR OUR "MORNING GLORY" GLASS.

(LEFT) AN EXAMPLE OF ONE OF OUR MOST BEAUTIFUL CUPS. BLUE BODY, DECORATED GOLD BAND AND THREE GOLD HANDLES.

COLLECTION OF FAVRILE GLASS. ITEM #1—SECOND PIECE OF LAMINATED GLASS MADE. ITEM #2—THE LAST PIECE OF GOLD LUSTER GLASS EVER MADE. ITEM #3—"CYPRIOTE" GLASS—EXPERIMENTAL PIECE. AUTHORS COLLECTION

COLLECTION OF FAVRILE GLASS. ITEM #1—THIS PIECE RECEIVED PARIS GOLD MEDAL AWARD IN 1910. ONLY PIECE OF IT'S KIND MADE. IT IS A FINE EXAMPLE OF CHEMICAL REACTIVE GLASS MADE JUST PRIOR TO OUR MORNING GLORY GLASS. ITEM #2—EXHIBITION PIECE—AN INVENTION OF ARTHUR J. NASH IN 1927. ENGRAVED LEAVES BETWEEN OPAL AND FLINT. ONLY PIECE OF IT'S KIND MADE. AUTHOR'S COLLECTION

COLLECTION OF FAVRILE GLASS. ITEM #1—REFERRED TO AS "THE PERFECT BLUE", THIS PIECE EXHIBITED MANY TIMES. ITEM #2—"SAMIAN" RED VASE RECEIVED PARIS GOLD MEDAL AWARD. THIS BEAUTIFUL RED GLASS WAS INVENTED BY ARTHUR J NASH. ITEM #3—AN EARLY FAVRILE VASE BY T. G. & D. CO. COLOR IS TRANSLUCENT BLUE WITH WHITE GARLANDS. AUTHOR'S COLLECTION

COLLECTION OF FAVRILE GLASS. ITEM #1—"SAMIAN" RED VASE—BLACK NECK DAMASCENED WITH GOLD. ITEM #2 (CENTER)—CAMEO VASE—EXHIBITION PIECE.— CARVED GREEN (CENTER) LEAVES, WITH REMAINING BODY CARVED THROUGH TO YELLOW. ITEM #3—EXHIBITION VASE OF TURQUOISE BLUE, DARK BLUE NECK WITH LIGHT BLUE DECORATION. AUTHOR'S COLLECTION

(LEFT) COLLECTION OF FAVRILE GLASS. ITEM #1—EXHIBITION VASE—MELON MOLDED— COLOR IS BLACK AND GREEN WITH GOLD FEATHERED DECORATION. ITEM #2— EXHIBITION VASE—BLUE LUSTER, HAS DARK BLUE-BLACK NECK WITH GOLD IRIDESCENT DECORATION. AUTHOR'S COLLECTION

COLLECTION OF FAVRILE GLASS. ITEM #1—VASE—EXHIBITION PIECE IN PARIS SALON 1900. HAND CUT ALL OVER, GREEN LEAVES AND WHITE FLOWERS. FLINT GLASS. ITEM #2—VASE—A BEAUTIFUL CHEMICAL REACTION. PIECE BY ARTHUR J NASH, 1905. EXHIBITION PIECE, COLOR IS YELLOW-GREEN LEAVES AND CHINESE RED. FIRST RED PRODUCED IN THIS PARTICULAR SHADE. ITEM #3—VASE—DEVITRIFIED OR SEMI-CRYSTALIZED GLASS. AN INVENTION OF LESLIE H NASH, AND WAS TO BE PRESENTED BY, THE LOUIS C. TIFFANY FURNACES INC., IN THE NEXT WORLD EXHIBITION. OPAL COLOR. AUTHOR'S COLLECTION

COLLECTION OF FAVRILE GLASS. ITEM #1—DEVITRIFIED OR SEMI-CRYSTALIZED GLASS VASE. AN INVENTION OF THE AUTHOR. THIS PIECE WAS TO BE PRESENTED, BY THE TIFFANY FURNACES INC., IN NEXT WORLD EXHIBITION. COLOR—INNER LACING THREADS OF GREEN AND BLUE, WITH INTERNAL BLAST OF GOLD IRIDESNENCE PRODUCING A JEWEL LIKE EFFECT. INNER LINING OF BLACK LUSTER. ITEM #2—COMPOTE—SPECIAL PIECE, AN INVENTION OF THE AUTHOR, BEAUTIFUL PEACOCK GREEN, WITH DAMASCENED BORDER. ITEM #3—VASE—DARK RED BODY, GREEN LEAVES, WITH CARVED WHITE FLOWERS. AUTHOR'S COLLECTION

COLLECTION OF FAVRILE GLASS. ITEM #1—VASE—APPLE GREEN WITH IRIDESCENT NECK DECORATION. ITEM #2—GLADIOLA VASE—REACTIVE GLASS—RECEIVED AWARDS AT ALASKA-YUKON EXHIBIT. COLOR-YELLOW GREEN LEAVES, WHITE FLOWERS, INTERNAL LUSTER. ITEM #3—VASE—EXHIBITION PIECE COLOR—INTERNAL TEXTURE OF MULTI COLORED FLAKES. AUTHOR'S COLLECTION

COLLECTION OF FAVRILE GLASS. ITEM #2—VASE—COLOR, A TEXTURE OF BLACK AND GOLD WITH GOLD DECORATION AROUND OPEN END. ITEM #3— MILLEFIORI—COLOR, CLEAR GREEN WITH WHITE FLOWERS. FLINT GLASS. ITEM #4— SMALL CAMEO VASE— EXHIBITION PIECE. ENTIRE SURFACE OF VASE IS CARVED. COLOR IS ORANGE ALL OVER. AUTHOR'S COLLECTION

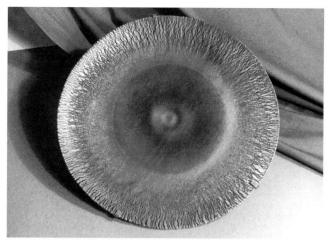

COLLECTION OF FAVRILE GLASS. ITEM #1—SMALL VASE—COLOR DARK GREEN AND LIGHT GREEN WITH INTERNEL FLAKES OF GOLD. ITEM #2—"CYPRIOTE" GLASS—EXPERIMENTAL PIECE. ITEM #3—SMALL VASE—COLOR OLIVE GREEN AND BLACK, WITH BEAUTIFUL DECORATION. AUTHOR'S COLLECTION

FAVRILE PLATE. BLUE AND GREEN IRIDESCENT SUNBURST PLATE

PARTIAL LIST OF AWARDS

Grand Prix Paris	1900
St. Petersburg	1901
Turin	1902
Gold Medal Buffalo	1901
Alaska—Yukon First Honorable Mention	1901
Paris Salon	1914
Gold Medal Panama-Pacific Exposition	1915

Eight early awards were given to Arthur J. Nash.

No awards earlier than 1900 were given for Favrile glass.

Many awards were made after 1915 some to the Company

Paris Salon, Place of honor Gold medal award 1921

The Museums listed below thought enough of FAVRILE glass to preserve it forever.[84]

Metropolitan Museum of Art	New York
Pratt Institute	Brooklyn, NY

Art Institute	Chicago
Field Columbian Museum	Chicago
National Museum	Washington
Carnegie Museum	Pittsburgh
Cincinnati Museum of Art	Cincinnati
Worcester Art Museum	Worcester
The Victoria and Albert Museum	London
Museum of Science and Art	Glasgow
Museum of Science and Art	Dublin
Musee du Luxembourg	Paris
Musee des Arts decoratifs	Paris
Musee Galliera	Paris
Musee du Conservstoire des Arts et Metiers	Paris
Musee de la Manufacture de Sevres	Sevres
Musee des Arts decoratifs	Limoges
Kunst Gewerbe Museum	Berlin
Musee des Arts Decoratifs	Bruxelles
Regio Museo Industriale	Turin
Museum fur Kunst and Gewerbe	Hamburg
Kestner Museum	Hanover
Museum of Decorative Arts	Dresden
Nordbohmisches Gewerbe Museum	Reichenberg
Kunst Gewerbe Museum	Leipzig
Kaiser Wilhelm Museum	Crefeld
Museum fur Kunst und Industrie	Vienna
Museum of Decorative Arts	Budapest
Museum of Copenhagen	Copenhagen
National Museum	Stockholm
Musee Stieglitz	St. Petersburgh
Musee de l'Ecole Central de Dessin	St. Petersburgh
Nordenfjeldske Kunstindustri Museum	Trondhjem

(TOP) SOME OF THE MEDALS RECEIVED BY ARTHUR J NASH PARIS
EXPOSITION UNIVERSELLE INTERNATIONAL 1900–PANAMA
PACIFIC EXPOSITION SAN FRANCISCO

(MIDDLE) AN AWARD RECEIVED BY ARTHUR J NASH, PARIS 1900

(BOTTOM) AWARD RECEIVED BY ARTHUR J NASH, PARIS 1900 . . .
SEVEN OTHER AWARDS WERE RECEIVED AT PARIS BY A. J. NASH.

Imperial Museum of Japan	Tokio, Japan
Museum of the Fine Arts Society	Tokio, Japan
The National Art Gallery of Victoria	Melbourne
Pennsylvania Museum and School of Industrial Art	Philadelphia, Pa
Musee des Arts Decoratifs	Bergen
Musee des Arts Decoratifs	Prague
Musee des Arts Industriels	Christiania
Imperial Commercial Museum	Tokio, Japan
An die Grossh Centralstelle fur die Gewerbe	Darmstadt
Musee de Mulhouse	Mulhouse

A LUXURY BUSINESS

After many years of working closely with my late father, I gradually took over many of his duties in the glass laboratory. It was only then as my responsibility increased that I realized the Glass business was no child's play. Chemistry in glass in its original form was quite simple but I soon found out that in our business it was the most complex thing I had ever been required to learn. Much of the Formula and processes were of a secret nature and could not be trusted with anyone else. With all my other duties I found my job rather taxing but enjoyable.

We were commissioned to make special glass by Kings, Queens, Princes, Emperors, and titled people, to say nothing of the great wealthy names in America. At most of the fashionable weddings you could see many pieces of FAVRILE glass in some form.

Golf, Polo, Tennis, Sailing and many of the sports awarded cups of FAVRILE glass at some time. Favrile glass was never cheap by comparison with other glass, in fact, I think it was the most expensive glass ever made. In many cases it was more costly than silver.

Its production (hand made) did not make for quantity, nor did we carry a large number of pieces of each kind. If you see a collection of FAVRILE Glass it would be surprising to find two pieces alike. Table glass or vases may be the exception because we carried name designs, such as: Prince, York, Merovignian, Queen, Dutchess, Royal Cypress and many others.

Only where talent and industry are rewarded can the highest standard of quality craftsmanship be maintained.

A business dedicated to art cares little for expense if in the end the objective has been realized. My father could not bear a failure, he was a perfectionist. I was brought up in this same manner but in later years I became conscious that after all in some forms of art to be perfect did not necessarily produce fine art. Creative art calls for daring. The creative mind works fast, therefore, if the product of your imagination becomes labored the result will lose its creative impact. Technical skill must come with years of practice. You cannot compose a symphony without a complete knowledge of music and I believe this is so in all creative arts. It takes years of study to interpret in any medium the concept of a moment when the wheels of creative thinking turn.

OTHERS TRY TO MAKE LUSTER

My constant worry was keeping all glass information secret. We had already suffered by some unscrupulous people on our payroll, who appeared trustworthy but going a little too far, they were discovered. Before they became wealthy they had lost vast sums of money trying to gain some information that would put them on top. No one has ever quite mastered the complex problem.

Two men died of disgrace and the third lost two fortunes of people he interested in the project. He was never quite able to perform. None of these people realized the enormous amounts of money required to carry on a business such as ours.

Also men versed in making our glass were not available. This in itself was a large handicap and of course the glass that was produced had no Art quality. There are a few pieces about but they are easy to recognize.

Our cross index of chemicals was confusing; as much as I used it I made an error now and then.[85] One number referred to another but mixed, not in order. For instance, a red 8 would refer to 13. Red representing deadly poison and 13 was arsenic. Transposing of numbers required constant care and attention.

Needle crystal antimony was 21 which referred you to 34. Very confusing. Anyone finding a slip of paper with a list of numbers might think this is it, but it would mean nothing more than a calender. In my notebook my private key was 21 + 13 when added = 34 = $H\,NO_3$. This was only used in the Laboratory. Now you have the secret, but I don't advise you to go into the glass business just yet.

THE BOOMER LOVING CUP

LUCIUS BOOMER LOVING CUP

The names on this cup are an exact duplication of the signatures of some of the most prominent names in the New York area.

The occasion was a banquet to honor Mr. Lucius Boomer, for his long active service as General Manager of the Waldorf Astoria Hotel, and later the Waldorf Hotel on Park Avenue.[86]

Mr. Boomer was host to some of the most distinguished guests visiting America. He was known the world over and was a very close friend of my Father, on many occasions I was invited to join them for luncheon. His experiences in the Hotel business were most interesting and entertaining. Mr. Boomer was very fond of "Favrile" Glass and used it extensively.

This particular banquet was held in the Biltmore Hotel. After a toast to Mr. Boomer the guests marched to a large urn and smashed the champagne glasses into it. All the broken glass sent to our factory and melted in the furnace.

The large loving cup made from this glass was about twelve inches in height, fashioned after the glasses used at the banquet. In the design, the windows and draped curtains were like those at the Biltmore.

At a later dinner Mr. Boomer was presented with this beautiful cup.

FAVRILE GLASS

90

(TOP) FAVRILE GLASS 1912 TO 1916

(MIDDLE) FAVRILE GLASS DESIGNED FOR EXPORT

(BOTTOM) FAVRILE GLASS THESE PICTURES WERE MADE IN GERMANY 1916; THE ONLY ONES I HAVE.

FAVRILE LAMPS

The stock of Tiffany lamps was extensive and comprised every form from the small desk lamp to the Mosaic floor standards. All of our lamps were of heavy bronze construction, of undoubted superiority and of artistic design.

The shades are of two kinds of Favrile glass blown in one piece after the manner of vases, or of pieces of glass bound together with copper and welded together, producing a result similar to the effect found in geometrical and floral windows.

The floral shades are particularly interesting, portraying in color the flowers they represent from the pastel tones of the magnolia and daffodil to the rich colors of the poppy, poinsettia and rose.

Many of you may remember the three eight-foot tall standards in the old Manhattan

(BELOW LEFT) FAVRILE TABLE LAMP. TABLE LAMP, BRONZE BASE INLAID VITREOUS ENAMEL SEVEN INCH ENGRAVED SHADE, LISTED AT $65.00 AUTHOR'S COLLECTION

(RIGHT) FAVRILE LAMPS $45.00 TO 60.00 BRONZE AND ENAMEL BASES PHOTOGRAPH FROM THE AUTHOR'S ALBUM.

Hotel. The shades were about thirty six inches in diameter and everyone talked about them. They created quite a sensation. The glass in these large shades was made especially for them and was of rare quality.

Lighting fixtures for public buildings, theatres, churches and high class residential and domestic fixtures *were* a large part of our business, all using Favrile glass.

The very large ceiling fixtures of bronze were made by the Tiffany Studios. We limited ourselves to table lamps and floor standards where Tiffany Favrile glass was the featured part.

TABLE LAMPS AND LIGHTING FIXTURES

Just about the time I started working with the Tiffany Furnaces, Inc. in the year 1908, oil lamps were being used and I can remember thinking how ugly they were. But the oil tank, wick and the chimney all had an important part to play in their design.

I started designing electric lamps,[87] this opened up a field of experiments and ideas which developed into a large part of our business. Leaded shades came into being and the studios were kept busy trying to keep up with the orders.

Then there were some unscrupulous people who tried to copy the shades. They were made out of glass that you could see in any cheap salon. They flooded the market, much to our disgust.

One of the big New York stores carried the thing too far, calling it Tiffany Tavorl. This ad cost them *a lawsuit* and took many of the shade makers out of the market. However, the damage was done.

This was a great shame because the leaded lamp shades made of Favrile glass were beautiful. Blown glass shades were never copied. The use of Favrile glass for lighting lasted until our factory closed.

FAVRILE TABLE LAMP. THIS LAMP IS A BEAUTIFUL COMBINATION OF METAL, GLASS AND POTTERY. LAMP BODY IS FAVRILE POTTERY, WITH METAL BASE. LEADED SHADE OF FAVRILE GLASS.[88] AUTHOR'S COLLECTION

FAVRILE-FABRIQUE

You may come across this name at sometime and wonder about it. The name was given to pressed forms used in lighting fixtures and lamp shades and represented silk in folds or sheared pleats.

An invention of mine—patented October 14th, 1913

You can see it used in Tiffany Studios lamp shades in amber and other colors. I used it for small shades on candle lamps and wall brackets. It is very effective and looks like real silk.

THE NON-REFILLABLE BOTTLE

In a newspaper was the following:

Notice to all concerned: $10,000 will be paid to anyone who can invent a bottle when once emptied, cannot be refilled.

I saw this problem and thought that it sounded rather foolish as I could not understand how they could fill the bottle in the first place. Therefore, I dismissed the idea entirely from my mind.

CALLED ON THE CARPET

I became very much interested in all kinds of inventions to make in glass, which were brought to us. Hardly a week passed without someone calling to have his idea made up.

It was customary for us to charge $1000.00 for carrying out ideas brought to us. This charge eliminated most of the would-be inventors.

Non-refillable bottles caused most of the trouble because $10,000 had been offered as a prize by a Whiskey firm. I filled them all by exhausting the air from the bottle and putting them under water which proved the point that they are refillable.

There were many more inventions, one of them was raised glass letters for signs, mounted in metal stencils and illuminated from behind a box.

Parabolic street lamps reflecting light from four sides—a clever thing but very expensive to make. This business became a headache.

There I was sitting before the Board of Directors accused of wasting my time and money. My answer was that out of this mess someone would have an idea which could make money for us. It did, the glass signs became a large business and produced large profit for the firm and it lasted for many years but was finally overcome when the Neon signs came out and took all the business.

New ideas can become very expensive to make and these adventures must be judged not for the moment but for a long range investment with a fair degree of certainty as to its success.

The profit made by glass letters more than covered any small loss sustained. They were used throughout the Grand Central Railroad Station in New York and all over the United States.

This profit turned out to be continuous for some years.

I knew what our expenses amounted to and believe me, they were heavy. There were times when loans had to be made. They were only of a temporary nature, however. This was the reason for doing things which were not in accordance with our aim which was to produce objects of Art. Through my many efforts, payrolls were met and there was seldom any financial trouble during slack seasons.

This effort finally brought about a better understanding between the Board and myself and later I was praised for my work in the company's behalf. None of these items ever bore any indication that they were made at our factory.

Somehow I was always involved in making all manner of things in glass, metal, enamel, etching, lighting fixtures or what have you. Anyway that was my job.

Mr. Tiffany would return from Europe filled with ideas.[89] No rest, no vacations, my brother in Nova Scotia and Dad in Europe. Everyone was away but me. I had no break for twelve years and finally I broke down. If people spoke to me, I started to cry. I thought it was the end. My Doctor sent me away alone and after a few weeks of golf in New England, I slowly regained my health and went back to work.

ENCHANTMENT—THE STORM

If you had the eye and brain of an artist, enchantment is the only word I can think of that could describe the picture I am about to portray.

The year is of no importance, however, it was one Monday morning in December. The men at that time of year were working day and night to complete Christmas orders. It had been snowing lightly all night and by seven o'clock in the morning there was a blanket of snow about five inches deep and the snow was still falling. The wind was rising and it bid fair to be a storm of some proportions. Louis Tiffany always made his weekly call promptly at eight o'clock every Monday morning. This morning I guess the Old Crain Simplex limousine could not get through. I was about ten minutes late as my little two-seater Hupmobile was having difficulty with a slipping clutch. Well, this was really it. The men were arriving one or two at a time with hats down, collars up, wearing boots and carrying dinner pails. Men at the factory were trying to shovel paths but were making no headway. The strong, chilly wind was rising and cut like a knife. I phoned my Dad not to attempt to come down. The trains on the Long Island Railroad were about half an hour late and getting worse. It looked like a stay over for those who had a distance to go. Now that is the first picture.

Upon entering the glass house I felt the welcome heat of the furnaces—all a red glow. I went back through the buildings to my studio which faced the north and took off my coat and rubbers. There was one thing for sure, I had to leave my studio as there was no heat and the north wind was impossible to endure. I returned to the comfort of the glass house. With the drone of the furnaces belching up heat at something over 2000 degrees, it was like summer—a wonderful dry heat that brought calm to your brain and comfort to your bones.

All about were the glass workers, blowing and gathering glass from the furnaces, swinging and tooling in their glassmakers chairs. Some were standing at gloryholes reheating their work. The annealing lehrs burning quietly, fired by coke, and over all the shop there was a warm yellow-orange light. The mens faces stood out against the dark walls and corners of the large iron building. It was a perfect *artists dream* if ever I saw one. I left this comfortable place to visit the other shops and found everyone suffering with cold. There was no heat in the buildings. On inspection I discovered that the night fireman had left but the day man who lived in Astoria had not shown up and the fires had gone out. It had to be on a day like this! I put another man on the job and in about an hour the blessed heat came in.

The day wore on. At dinner time I sent out for ten large steaks, potatoes, bread and butter, apples, beer, wine and coffee.

The Lehr is a long oven about 80 feet with iron pans about 36 inches wide and about four feet long linked together. It moved somewhat like a conveyor in a tunnel with a coke fire under the forward end. This device is used for annealing the glass (relieving the strain.) For frying steak there is nothing that can compare with it. The smell of coffee and steak on that frightful night was heavenly. The men sang songs, told stories and laughter was provoked by the stimulus of wine and beer and a warm friendly feeling prevailed in the glass house. The men worked until two o'clock in the morning filling all their orders. They slept on benches in the hallways covered with their overcoats but not one man complained. I think the party and work in the warm factory contributed to exhaustion but in the morning they were as fresh as usual.

I myself had little sleep. I tried my Dad's leather chair in his office but almost broke my neck and finally about five o'clock in the morning I gave up and made some coffee which brought me back to life.

The storm was over and by noon things started to look a bit more normal but no transportation of any kind moved. Two days later things began to move and the sun came out and made many beautiful pictures. There is never a dull moment in the glass business.

MEN IMPROVE—WITH HALF A CHANCE

I was just thinking about men. I have worked with men all my business life and have had many experiences with them. I have come to the conclusion that the men who worked in the Tiffany plants, numbering over a thousand at times, were the finest men it has been my privilege to come in contact with. They were of high caliber, understanding, respectful, unselfish and cared for the welfare of their fellow workers. They worked hard and if we were pressed for time on a contract, they would deliver before the due date. They were dependable and in return got respect from their foremen and bosses. They also received a generous bonus when business was good. They held fast to this high standard required of them. Our name stood for quality.

During my early training in Civil Engineering and eighteen months in Europe studying Art, I took up architectural engineering. My work started at the Terminal warehouse at West 28th St. and 11th Avenue. Many of you will remember Death Avenue with the freight trains running in the street on 11th Avenue. Also the 28th and 29th Street horse cars about the year 1907 and the Belt Line.

It was a mean job, pulling out old steam elevators and installing generators and electric elevators and lighting in the cold storage for Siegel & Cooper, Charles & Co., Macy, Wanamaker and dozens of others.

THE NIGHT ENGINEER MAKES AN ERROR

Lets just call him Joe. Joe was the night engineer and Henry was the night watchman. It was the duty of the Engineer to check the oil level in the large storage tanks in the factory yard, every four hours and also the pressure at the burners of both air and oil.

The float on the end of a chain with a counter weight ran over a pulley above the oil tank. When the engineer made his inspection the telltale marker was not in sight. He became alarmed and thought the tank was empty. It was a bad night, wind and rain, and the yard was in darkness. The engineer went back to the engine room and got a lantern. I forgot to mention that he had a rather heavy beard and mustache.

I awakened early the next morning and decided to go to the plant and arrived about 6:45 A.M. I walked across the yard to my office. Shortly after, there was a knock at my door. I said "Come in" and a complete stranger stood before me. I said, "Well, sir, do you wish to see me?" He answered in the affirmative and I asked "Who are you and what do you want?" I noticed the back of his head and arms were severely burned. I was amazed at the sight.

I said, "You are injured, tell me quickly what's the trouble?" "Well, sir, I am Joe, the night engineer. I went to check the oil last night and the telltale float had come off the chain. I thought I might get it with a long pole but I could not see it, so I got a lantern and rope and dropped it down the manhole of the tank. The explosion was terrible. The flame shot up about 60 feet with a loud report. I was blown across the yard and landed in the pea coal bin which was lucky for me. I rushed and put oil all over me but I gotta see a Doctor. The whole town was down here and nobody saw me. I had been there for over an hour."

I took him in my car to the Doctor who fixed him up. He was in great pain and did not return to work for two weeks. The reason I did not know him was that just every bit of his beard and hair were burned off.

The moral of this story is:

If you are not sure about how much gas you have in your gas tank don't light a match to find out. Just turn your car upside down.

MOSAICS

Glass Mosaic was first used for floors, as a medium for mural surface decoration. It had its growth and decay from the time of Constantine to the early part of the fourteenth century A.D. It was revived at Venice in 1838 and has since continued to regain its former position in the Art of Europe.

As far back as 1879 Mr. Tiffany employed it in the decoration of the Union League Club of New York. Mr. Tiffany has been an ardent advocate of its use, on account of its color-decorative possibilities, its effectual resistance of the corrosion of natural and artificial decay and its retention of its pristine beauty; it being non-absorbent, fireproof, and practically indestructable.

In Mr. Tiffany's earnest desire to have more color in his Mosaics, he found difficulty in obtaining the colors. This was one reason why he made a wide search for just the right man who had the knowledge to produce the glass he desired.

This was where Mr. Nash came into the picture. The beautifying material of all Tiffany Mosaics was the product of Mr. Nash's many years of experience in glass, the thing which added richness in color and beauty to the final concept.

These two men belonged together if Art was their goal and I am sure that it was.

DREAM GARDEN

"THE DREAM GARDEN" MOSAIC IN
FAVRILE GLASS—MEASURES 49 × 15
FEET. DESIGNED BY MAXFIELD PARISH
FOR THE CURTIS PUBLISHING CO.—
EXECUTED BY THE TIFFANY STUDIOS,
SUPERVISED BY LOUIS C. TIFFANY.

[On] this page you will see a picture called "The Dream Garden." It is a Mosaic made of all kinds of glass from luster to opal and hundreds of various colors. As I remember, it was forty nine feet long and fifteen feet high. It was made for the Curtis Publishing Company in Philadelphia, Pennsylvania. It was designed by Maxfield Parish and executed in <u>FAVRILE</u> glass by the Ecclesiastical Department of the Tiffany Studios, under the careful supervision of Mr. Tiffany. It was on exhibition in New York for one month.[90]

The glass used in this Mosaic was my headache and it took me almost two and one half years to make. Flat glass had been turned over to me by my Dad with all its complications and in this job, there were many.

It is an amazing thing and can only be properly appreciated by a visit. There is a surprise in store for you. I am sure you will enjoy this magnificent piece of work. It was one of our most important Mosaics and a credit to all who worked on it. Mr. Tiffany gave the final word of approval with Mr. Parish, who I understand, was delighted. The picture in this book is through the kindness of the Curtis Publishing Company.

MEXICAN THEATRE CURTAIN MOSAIC

Flanked by the great organ of 7000 pipes, the Mosaic representing Sciences and Arts contains over 1,000,000 small pieces of Favrile glass executed by the Tiffany Studios of

New York. This curtain is supported in a steel frame and weighs 21 tons. It is raised by a special elevating device operated by two motors.

Its visible altitude is forty six feet and represents the Valley of Mexico and was designed by the Mexican artist, Dr. Atl. The Mosaic was installed about 1922, if memory serves me correctly.[91]

The making of the glass for this wonderful Mosaic took almost three years and kept me working many days and nights. There are hundreds of various colors shown.

The curtain was on exhibition for one month in the studios on Madison Ave. and literally thousands of people came to view it. We all were proud to have contributed to this masterful work of art.

The exterior dome was to be covered with iridescent glass so that it could have been seen for miles but the cost was so high that it was abandoned.

The curtain was so important to us that no book on Favrile glass could be written without mention of it.

EARLY STAINED GLASS WINDOWS

Little is known of the origin and early history of the Art of painting on glass and of the manufacture of the colored materials.

It is a fact that stained or colored glass is an accessory to all ecclesiastical edifices, and in attempting to portray the sufferings of our Saviour, the lives of the Apostles, Martyrs and the Holy Men, who have devoted themselves to Christianity, nothing has been found more effective than the stories and incidents portrayed in glass by painted pictures. It subdues and chastens excessive light and concentrates the mind to one devotional purpose.

Mosaics, stained glass murals and understanding artists probably gave more to the world than anything I can think of. They gave to the people in pictures the things they could not read for the simple reason there were no books to read, at least very few.

The French claim the invention of stained glass windows and taught the English who in turn taught the Germans. It was thought that painted and stained glass was a lost art and known by only a few. This is not correct, for it is true that in modern days, the knowledge of colors, enamels and glass making is far greater than the ancient glass makers ever attained. It can be seen in porcelain, china, enamels and glass.

I could go on for a long time telling you where these windows can be seen but it has all been said many times.

One thing I found out was that glass windows did not appear in England until 1248. This was important because in one book, I read that stained glass appeared only a few years before this date in France.

The earliest examples of this Art were made in the Ninth Century. Some of them remain in the aisles of Canterbury Cathedral and in Europe in the year 1248 in the King's rescript.

All this long research helped me very little in making colors because there were no samples to go by. However, some fairly good work was accomplished but only for a short time. When the Tiffany windows became known they were in constant demand and will probably go down in history as a new method of making windows in Favrile glass.

There was little or no variation to the reds and blues in early glass. They were just plain pieces of glass. This is understandable because the glass used for staining was cut from a sheet like any ordinary glass found in a window today.

In Favrile glass the effect is broken up by varying thickness or the addition of another color combined during its rolling on the table. This effect produced is an advance in window making. Opalescent in mottled effects adds also to the play of light admitted.

One more advance in Favrile windows is that each section is bound on the edges with copper and then soldered—making a tight joint. Less expensive windows are put together with chanell lead, like the letter "H". This would be impossible in our windows due to the varying thickness.

In the early church windows in which you see stained glass used, silver, copper and

Adoration of the Magi
by Louis C. Tiffany
Centre panel of Chancel Window
in Christ Church, Brooklyn, N.Y.

"The Earth is the Lord's
and the fullness thereof."
Memorial Landscape Window
by Louis C. Tiffany

cobalt, played an important part in obtaining the colors. Their problems were many. After analyzing fragments of the old glass, I discovered that there was still much to be desired, but these early window makers deserved a great deal of credit for their accomplishments.

CHURCH WINDOWS[92]

Having been associated with Art all my life and having made a study of oil painting, I discovered many times that the medium used in the production of Art had much to do with the result.

When in Europe my Father took me to the churches and cathedrals to see the stained glass windows. Dad would tell me that people who attended church in the past, could neither read nor write and it was through stained glass windows, Mosaics and paintings that the underprivileged people gained knowledge of the Bible. From some of the windows I saw, I did not see how it was possible to gain much religious knowledge from them. Of course there were many beautiful windows which were very inspiring.

I think Louis C. Tiffany was somewhat affected by this, lets say abstract rendering and preferred to make his windows with more realism, opalescent landscape effects.

Mr. Frederick Wilson, our top window designer with whom I had many discussions was of the opinion that no one depicting religious figures had much to go on other than description. He also thought that misunderstanding was displayed in the early windows. He told me that he had made hundreds of drawings of Christ and every one was different. In some of his work the head would be rendered in shadow or turned in an unrecognizable position. On the other hand Mr. Tiffany was the critic and made many changes in his windows. I have seen him look at a finished window and then tear it all to pieces making so many changes that the original design was completely lost.

This all came home to me when I was called in to make color changes in glass. This I think was my big headache. Almost every window was made twice. I hated it. It seemed impossible that to permit a piece of work to advance that far without correction was very poor management, but that was Mr. Tiffany's way. It happened to me many times but if the drawings were right for production no one on earth could get me to change them. Perhaps I was stubborn. On the other hand I had so much to do that I just couldn't spare the time. My attitude became tough as time went on. With me it was like it or pitch it. To play around for weeks was exhausting to say the least. As my Father used to say, "Touch and retouch until all be ripe or rotten."

However, we turned out, to say nothing of expense, some wonderful windows which received much praise and admiration. For my part the selection of color was carried out with the utmost care by men competent and experienced in this field of Art.

I should like to mention five men who excelled in the making of church windows:

SIR BURNE-JONES	ENGLISH
LOUIS C. TIFFANY	AMERICAN
HENRY HOLLIDAY	AMERICAN
FREDERICK WILSON	AMERICAN
ARTHUR J. NASH	ENGLISH

"Whose glass has contributed so much to the
richness of leaded windows."

In their windows I am happy to say the effect of a kalidescope never enters my mind as it did while viewing many church windows in Europe, not all, but many that I saw did, especially the Rose and Medallion windows.

In Sir Burne-Jones designs I have the feeling of drapery more than that of the subject matter, but I think his period had much to do with this. The figures in his later windows, I am not sure of the date, have some painted parts but the drapery throughout is simple, with larger masses, and at a distance a somewhat darker background seems to lend dignity. The mass of lead lines is sharply cut down. His stylized figures with small hands and faces are quite typical of his work. The strength of the face appears lost many times by weak painting and its proportion to the figure. Many of his windows require better glass.

The window in Jesus College Chapel, Cambridge, England, designed by Sir E. Burne-Jones shows a reserve in color. Of course he had his problems in glass along with many others.

As far as Tiffany windows are concerned they never suffered for the want of fine glass. On the other hand I have seen some wonderful early windows in Europe. I only wish that more information was available on them. But glass color has been their problem. I am glad to say that we were able to overcome these problems which must have disappointed the early designers.

<u>Henry Holliday</u>: I never had the pleasure of meeting Mr. Holliday although during my twenty three years of making flat glass for Mr. Tiffany I met many prominant people. I always had great respect for Mr. Holliday's masterful drawing. His work in many fields was a pleasure to see. I often felt that I would like to help him in his glass problems, there are many I can assure you, not in his windows alone. Red is the big problem.

My Father, Arthur J. Nash, having made glass for Powells of London and Chances, knew the many pitfalls of glass making but being a master chemist in glass he "always came up with the answers."

The aesthetic side of Mr. Holiday's windows is outstanding. I have always admired his work. I can not help adding his name to the list, I somehow feel that he would not mind.

In years of experiment and accomplishment there was no man that worked harder to gain respect in the art of creating church windows and mosaics than Louis C. Tiffany. He was fortunate in having my Father to help him with his glass problems. This was Mr. Tiffany's reason for inviting my Father to come to America.

Mr. Frederick Wilson, designer for Tiffany Studios was a wonderful person in his field, a true artist and a masterful designer, one of the best. His figures were supreme.

Tiffany FAVRILE Glass was first made for Church windows in 1892 by Arthur J. Nash, Vice President of the Louis C. Tiffany Furnaces, Inc., and later by his two sons A. D. Nash and L. H. Nash.

The windows were made by the Ecclesiastical Department of the Tiffany Studios under the close supervision of Mr. Tiffany.

The following is a partial list of the famous FAVRILE GLASS WINDOWS:

TWO EARLY WINDOWS, SHOWING THE CAREFUL USE OF LEAD LINES. THIS BLACK AND WHITE, IS A COPY FROM A BADLY FADED PICTURE. BY MY SON JOHN W. NASH. ORIGINAL DESIGN BY FREDERIC WILSON.

PARTIAL LIST OF FAVRILE GLASS WINDOWS

Memorial Andrew Carnegie—last survivor of his family

Landscape erected in Dunfermline, Scotland in the Abbey

Memorial to English Martyrs "Roman Catholic"

Memorial to Stoddard First Presbyterian Church, Dayton, Ohio

Memorial to Russell Sage, First Presbyterian Church, Far Rockaway, L.I., N.Y.

Memorial to Marsh St. Paul's Church, Patterson, N.J. The river of the Water of Life

Figure King Soloman Window—Kane Lodge No. 45A Masonic Chapel, Utica, N.Y.

Figure Window to Stillman Memorial, Church of the Messiah, Brooklyn, N.Y.

Memorial Windows to A.K.P. Dennett & F.P. Morris, Baptist Church, Flushing, N.Y.

Sketch Figure Window by Wilson Favrile glass Twelve Apostles, the Christ Child, Mary and Angels

Window—A beautiful window to see. Metropolitan Museum, N.Y. City The Elevation of Our Lord

Memorial to Charles H. Tyler Gutenberg taking first impression from movable type press, Winchester, Mass. Public Library Memorial

Tablet Sketch Memorial—Mosaic, carved marble inlaid Favrile glass

Residence Window R.B. Mellon—Landscape Favrile Glass

Domestic For Town House of J.R. DeLamar, N.Y. City

Mosaic—Curtain for Mexican Capitol Theatre—20 tons Mosaic made of iridescent glass. (Must be seen to be appreciated.)

Mosaic Panel—Chancel Unitarian Church at New Bedford, Massachusetts

Mosaic—The Dream Garden designed by Maxfield Parish Luster glass <u>Favrile</u> forty nine feet × twelve feet

Marble inlaid glass entire altar and pulpit placed in St. Michaels Protestant Episcopal Church—99th Street cor Amsterdam Ave. N.Y.C.

Font Inlaid Sienna Marble Favrile Glass Reformed Church, Albany, N.Y.

Mosaic Favrile glass All Angels Chapel of St. Michael and All Angels Church New York City by Wilson *and LCT*

Mosaic Memorial Christ Church, Brooklyn, N.Y. and many others of a high order.

SKETCH FOR FAVRILE GLASS MEMORIAL WIDOW TO ENGLISH MARTYRS. MADE BY THE TIFFANY STUDIOS.

I do not know of Mr. Spear's whereabouts but I am sure he would approve of my using his beautiful poem.[93] It almost tells my story.

GLORY TO THEM

"Glory to them the toilers of the earth
Who wrought with knotted hands in wood, glass and stone
Dreams their unlettered minds could not give birth
And symmetries their souls had never known.
Glory to them the artisans, who spread
Cathedrals like brown lace before the sun
Who could not build a rhyme, but reared instead
The Doric grandure of the Parthenon,
I never cross a marble Portico
Or lift my eyes where stained glass windows steal
From Virgin sunlight moods of deeper glow
Or walk down peopled streets, except to feel
A hush of reverence for that vast dead,
Who gave us beauty for a crust of bread."

BY ANDERSON M. SPEAR

This beautiful poem covers many of my thoughts with relation to Art. My compliments to Mr. Spear. It is with reverence that I use his poem.

CHURCH WINDOWS

To interpret and create pictures from religious discriptions found in the Bible is one of the most difficult things to do.

Rapheal to me, was supreme in his paintings, he felt and believed everything he did, to see his work gives the observer a desire to thank him for his works of Art.

To gain this celestial beauty in windows is a problem for the glass maker.

All of you have seen windows in gaudy colors and designed by men, who unlike Rapheal, I am sorry to say, reflect the desire of the maker, to be a little more frugal when buying glass, and the result often produces a disquieting effect in the window, subtle qualities are lost.

The diaphanous effect of Angels wings is non-existant, the destroying of folds in the drapery by heavy lead lines have no relation to form or composition of the whole, and in almost all cases, the glass appears vivid.

The "Crocketing" or border, is often too strong for the subject matter. All these things received careful attention in the Tiffany Favrile windows.

There are three kinds of colored glass windows.

Enamel glass—small, very beautiful, seldom made today.

Stained glass—used in early windows.

Pot Metal-glass colors made in the melting furnace.

In all Favrile glass windows, the color was an intergral part of the glass—stain was used only in the faces, hands, and feet.

I fully realize that windows makers found it impossible to get the kind of glass used in Favrile glass windows. There are some people who would rather see the earlier type of glass windows. On the other hand, progress in chemistry and a clearer understanding give beauty and better interpretation of religious history.

It is my hope that the creation of church windows will continue for many years. Periods will change in designs and color, but the subject matter will remain for Artists to interpret.

(TOP) A FAVRILE GLASS WINDOW "KING SOLOMON" MADE BY TIFFANY STUDIOS. PRODUCED FOR KANE LODGE NO. 454 AND PLACED IN THE MASONIC CHAPEL AT UTICA, NEW YORK.

(BOTTOM) A PUBLIC LIBRARY MEMORIAL WINDOW "THE FIRST PRINTING" GUTENBERG TAKING FIRST IMPRESSION FROM MOVEABLE PRESS. MEMORIAL TO HON. CHARLES H. TYLER (PUBLIC LIBRARY, WINCHESTER, MASS.)

THE ECCLESIASTICAL DEPARTMENT

The Ecclesiastical Department of the Tiffany Studios was located on 23rd Street. In this Department there was on display everything for the church in all denominations. These

included Communion tables, Baptismal fonts, crosses, altar cloths, candlesticks, single and seven branch candlesticks, votive candle cups, collection trays, robes for every purpose, entire Mosaic altars, chancel and pulpits, bronze tablets in memorium, carpets and rugs, church windows, Mosaic murals and many more objects too numerous to mention.

When you entered the many rooms everyone whispered and with so many heavy drapes it was almost impossible to hear what was said. A deep religious feeling came over our visitors.

It was here that Louis C Tiffany had his studio where he did much of his painting. He seldom saw or talked with customers and if he did, it was very briefly, merely an introduction.

Knowing him so well, I think he enjoyed being with me in my studio at the factory. With me he was happy and laughed—sometimes at the things I made from his drawings. They were at times, rather difficult and no matter what I did for him he would change it. I would then make the change and all was lost in utter confusion. So we would try again and again.

I liked doing things for him, after all I only saw him for about half-an-hour every Monday morning. But if he asked me to make up one more fountain, Oh, Boy! I thought I would go mad.

On one occasion I was making a clock for him. It took three years to make and I think he got tired of it but I made every single change he wanted and finally the clock was put on sale at Tiffany & Co. and remained there until our business closed. The time sheet showed 652 hours of work and the foundry had a charge of $142.00.

Yes, it was difficult to make money in a business like ours.

THE RUSSELL SAGE MEMORIAL WINDOW AT ROCKAWAY, L.I., N.Y.

The window was quite large. If I remember it was about 18 ft. high and 12 ft. wide. The subject was an old tree bent by the insistent south winds growing near the marsh land and dunes. The sun set was just about in its last stages with rich reds, pink, blue, green, violet, and others.

The glass in this window was made in large pieces composed of from four to six colors in a single sheet. To make this glass is a problem in chemistry. Each of the five colors must be adjusted to shrink exactly the same when cooling or the sheet would shatter into bits.

We had often put three colors together and even a fourth which may have been a thread but five and six presented a problem. However, many experiments finally gave us what we required. It is rather an unusual landscape window but knowing Long Island as I do, to me it is a beautiful thing.

Mrs. Sage thought it was fitting. The church was, I believe, built by Mr. Sage and endowed by him but most of the members have died or moved away and I have heard that the congregation has shrunk to a very few. However, the window is well worth a visit.

THE RUSSELL SAGE MEMORIAL WINDOW. TIFFANY FAVRILE GLASS FAR ROCKAWAY, L.I. N.Y.

MUCH OF THE CHARM OF EARLY WINDOWS WASHES OFF

Many times during my life I have wondered why certain things are made. Art expressed in many ways gives satisfaction in some way to its creator but why should I admire it? Certainly so far I have not been convinced when looking at some modern painting of today.

And don't say that I don't understand it. I saw the craze start when _Cezanne_ closed the old book and started on a fresh page. Picasso and the rest started going down hill at a fast pace. There are exceptions of course, and change is essential to progress.

But I somehow don't feel that going down hill will prove anything. In the early church stained glass windows you see colors which you wouldn't dare to use today. _The size of the pieces of glass were responsible for ugliness in design._ Lead lines across the face and other parts did not add to its beauty. Materials were responsible for most of this. It was not entirely the fault of the artist but many students think all that was intended. The 12th and 13th century period of windows were the finest as many agree. During World War I much destruction took place in France. Later a small Cathedral window was purchased by Mr. Tiffany. This window had been written about before the war and mention was made of the wonderful color in the glass.

I was looking at this small window one day with Mr. Tiffany and he asked me what I thought of it. I had just finished reading his clipping about it. "Well" I said, "that window is so dirty that it is hard to tell what the original glass looked like."

About a week later I was in town and saw the window again. Mr. Tiffany had washed half of the window. It had lost the mellow effect and the shading near the lead lines, and become a common place thing.

I have gone into Cathedrals and churches abroad and wondered what it was that gave these windows their charm. Later I discovered that years of burning candles inside, and smoke and dust outside, had mellowed the color of the glass and reduced the hard contrast. I was given a few fragments of the very old glass which gave proof as mentioned. I also discovered that glass fades in the strong sunlight but today that condition has been taken care of.

THE REVERBERATORY PROCESS

Reverberatory coloring used by us was not know at that time and I have no evidence of it having been used by anyone else. It is a process of, lets say, two large flower pots put into a furnace of special design. One pot has clear glass, the other has strong color. When the materials melt at high temperature the fuming of the materials effect one another and the clear glass takes on the color of the other in beautiful tints.

I discovered this reverberatory effect when glazing some pottery. One piece had a red glaze and the other ivory. After firing to Cone-9, I examined them and decided to do some more, but only carrying the heat to Cone-7. I found more heat was required.

Looking back at the first pieces, I discovered that one side of the ivory piece was pink. I could not understand this because I had put the glaze on myself. I talked it over with Dad and he thought that reverberatory action had taken place. We tried other colors and the same thing happened but the best results occurred at Cone-9, high temperature.

This led to further experiments. I designed a furnace to hold three pots, each of about 150 pounds capacity. The glass was prepared and put into the large open pots. The results were amazing and after many experiments with glass, we were able to get uniform control. Three colors were successfully carried out, improvements were made in the furnace and many wonderful things were made—sometimes two and three colors were used.

Dad told me that this had been done on chinaware in England but poor control was the cause of abandoning it.

NOW I MAKE CHURCH WINDOW GLASS

Although I became associated with our business in 1908, working in many of the departments, It was about 1912 that my father sent for me and said, "Leslie, this year I am turning over the flat glass and all it entails to you, you will use my formula until you become familiar with the laboratory work. You will experience many difficulties but you can always call upon me for help." That was my start in glass making.

In doing this, I knew that I would come into closer contact with the Ecclesiastical Department. When watching church window glass being made, a feeling often came over me that this glass must be the best. It was important.

Favrile glass forms the basic part of all Tiffany Windows after 1893. It is easy to identify, these windows have a distinctive appearance not found in other windows. Floral and landscape effects appear frequently, and great dignity is expressed at all times.

The drapery for figures is rolled and formed into natural folds by hand on the table. Feather drapery is made by moving the roller by hand back and forth a short distance. This creates a feather appearance. Ripple glass used in water effects is formed by rolling the glass on a moving table of iron. The roller is made to rotate faster than the table moves thus creating ripples in the glass.

Some windows were made entirely of glass including hands, feet and faces which heretofore have always been painted and fired. The glass for faces is made in five layers from shadow to highlight and then acid etched to produce the face, hands and feet.[94]

This is something new for windows, never having been done before to my knowledge. There was no such thing as good enough in our glass, it had to be perfect.

To make fine windows requires top designers, cutters, glazers, and many other artisans with years of experience in the field of window making. And I add, to say nothing of the fellow who produces the glass.

Very little stain or enamel was used. The wealth of color gradations in the glass gives the artisan the power to interpret the cartoon. No part of the development of a Tiffany window can be done mechanically. The design is interpreted in the spirit of Art. Even the leading is made to assist the design which was formally effected by paint. There is sincerity in all this, which makes for real Art.

I really realized that my responsibility was great, also that the many hazzards to overcome were paramount in this work, where, literally hundreds of changes must be made no matter how difficult it became.

Getting just the right tint, tone or shade could not be done as you might do when painting a picture. Each color had to be made separately. Sometimes you would make the color five times to meet the requirements which were so exacting. Slowly, I became quite proficient in this work and my art training proved to be very beneficial.

I soon realized why Dad wished to be relieved of this tiring never ending type of work. It was not as interesting to me as I expected because I seldom saw how it was being used. I could not spare the time to go into the city.

A discouraging thing to me also was having to make up 500 lbs. of glass, then the man would come to the factory and select one sheet and we had to put the rest into stock. It may never be called for again. Our cellars were jammed packed with glass that probably would never see the light of day. I could have sold all of it to the trade but L. C. Tiffany never permitted a square inch to be sold. It was all reserved for his windows—a great loss to us.

Whenever my phone rang the request was always the same, "We would like you to make." I always cut them off by saying that there is plenty in stock, come and select it. They hated this job because I made them pay for breakage which happened almost every time when pulling out sheets of glass.

I have accumulated hundreds of formulae for flat glass with variations of only a fractional change giving a different shade of color. Prior to my taking over the flatglass there was no record or index of what was in stock. In order to select a color you had to go through many racks to find the piece you wanted. This I changed so that you could find the color you wanted in minutes instead of hours. This alone saved a lot of work also it prevented duplication.

The cost of leaded windows depends on the number of figures used. These windows would cost from $40.00 per square foot and may go to $75 to $100 or more. Medallion and rose windows could go to Almost any price.

Landscape windows ran from $30. per square foot up to $50. All these prices depended largely on the subject and the type of glass used. If experimental or special colors were used, the price would go very high.

It is difficult to estimate the cost of leaded glass windows and to make the glass was a constant challenge. My hair is now snow white and I am sure that it was making flat glass that started it.

Joseph Briggs and E. E. Hayward supervised the making of the windows.

SAMIAN RED GLASS[95]

This celebrated pottery of the Romans was made at Arretium (Modern Arezzo). The paste is close and fine and of a rich red with a glaze so thin as to be almost *in*distinguishable.

It was extensively used for domestic purposes as well as for ornaments. The decoration consisted of fine mouldings in relief. Often names are found on it "Bibe Amice de Meo" ("Friend drink with me"). This ware was held in high estimation by the Romans and became priceless, few pieces exist today.

Their magnificient colors gave inspiration to Arthur J. Nash. Knowing the many pitfalls of producing red glass, he nevertheless wanted to prove to himself that this wonderful Samian red could be produced. It was finally made a year or two after I joined the Company, about *1911*.[96]

I am happy to say that I have two pieces of this wonderful color. It was very expensive. (See Photograph [on p. 84]) Very few of these vases were made. Mr. Tiffany thought that to decorate with leaves would improve it but Dad preferred only the plain red. My Father said, "I will try a piece but the green will not stand up on the red," it did not. However, some decoration was used on neck bands with fair success.

MR. TIFFANY'S EGYPTIAN PARTY

I can tell very little about the party other than the fact that it was a great success.[97] The only reason I mention it is to tell you about the Champagne glasses. Normally, a champagne glass has a hollow leg and keeps the wine bubbling and adds a festive appearance to a dinner party.

Mr. Tiffany came to me one morning and explained that he wanted a champagne glass that would bubble up not in one place but four. I worked on it for about a week and finally came up with it. It was a delicate shade of green with a blush of luster. Here it is;

I have one glass in my collection but what happened to the other 500 which were made? I have never come across one anywhere. It is quite possible that they were smashed into an urn after the toast. This has been done many times.

METAL COMBINED WITH GLASS

You will notice in many cases the use of metal work as an aid in producing some remarkable effects. The sketch shows a copper chalice. The design is etched clear through and glass of various colors was blown into the cups and extending through the openings and gave the effect of inlaid sections. It was then gold plated.

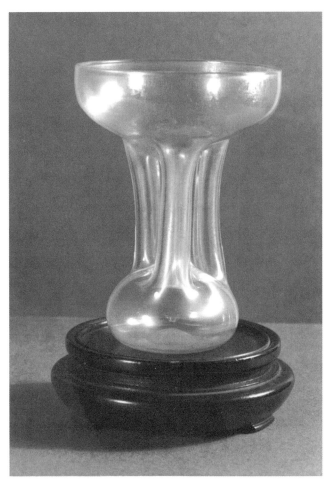

CHAMPAGNE GLASS MADE FOR MR. TIFFANY FOR HIS EGYPTIAN PARTY. BUBBLES RISE UP IN FOUR HOLLOW STEMS. FROM THE AUTHOR'S COLLECTION

I discovered the inspiration for this type of work in the Albert Museum in Birmingham, England. It was of Spanish origin made by their famous goldsmiths of the sixteenth century. I think from other things that I saw that I was impressed with the idea that this type of work was done by Benevenuto Cellini. He represented the gold, silversmiths and jewelers as the revival of Michael Angelo and Raphael represent the painters.

I think Italian goldsmiths were so fine that they should be included. Germany did some work of this kind but it was never equal to Spain.

The sketch was made of silver, and the inlays were gold. Twisted frames of wire were made; with glass, blown inside to give a similar effect. We introduced the blowing of glass into the *apertures,* blue and gold were my favorite. You may find tall candlesticks, lamps, vases, and now and then, boxes done after this method.

Reticulated Glass.

la guage
Etched copper

Soft bronze

Cast bronze

metal

glass

Early Oil lamp.

Wire

Metal and glass combined.

FAVRILE METALWORK

With

Vitreous Enamels

Desk Sets—Paper racks, bookends, paper knives, blotters, blotter ends, Scales, stamp
    boxes, pen trays and desk clocks.

Bowls—Plain and etched.

Trays—Plain and etched

Boxes—Cigarette, Cigar and candy—etched, enameled and plain.

Desk Lamps—Many kinds, glass shades—enamel bases.

Floor Lamps—Many kinds—enamel on copper gauze shades.

Reading Lamps—Swing shades adjustable light

Some articles in pewter after Paul Revere.

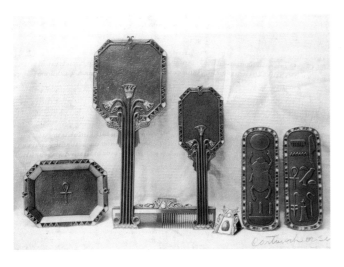

THIS BUREAU SET WAS IN ENAMEL, COPIED FROM FRAGMENTS FOUND IN KING TUTANKERMAN TOMB. DESIGNED BY LESLIE H. NASH. FOR MRS. CYRUS McCORMACK. THE METAL WAS MADE OF PURE COPPER. THE HAND MIRROR WAS POLISHED COPPER.

BRONZE AND ENAMEL FAVRILE CLOCKS BY LESLIE H. NASH [98]

FAVRILE BLUE LUSTER BOX. METAL FRAMED BOX HAS BLUE LUSTER GLASS PANELS. DESIGNED BY THE AUTHOR. AUTHOR'S COLLECTION

ENAMELED METAL BOX THIS GOLD PLATED ENAMELED BOX, INSPIRED BY AN EARLY AMERICAN OAK CHEST IN THE AMERICAN WING OF THE METROPOLITAN MUSEUM, WAS DESIGNED BY THE AUTHOR, AND RECEIVED AWARD OF MERIT AT CHICAGO FINE ARTS EXHIBITION, AS A PRODUCT OF THE LOUIS C. TIFFANY FURNACES INC. AUTHOR'S COLLECTION [99]

COLLECTION OF VITREOUS ENAMELS THESE EARLY PIECES WERE MADE BY TIFFANY GLASS & DECORATING CO.—THE ENTIRE SURFACE OF EACH PIECE IS ENAMELED. ITEMS #1 AND #4 ARE INK WELL STANDS, AND THE DESIGN IS FORMED IN COPPER BY THE REPOUSSÉ METHOD. AUTHOR'S COLLECTION.

Elevator Doors—Inlaid luster glass—etched and enameled. Many odd pieces too numerous to mention.

Enamel pieces of copper, hammered, spun into boxes, trays, ornamental pieces mostly small. All metal with one exception *copper* was mostly cast bronze, some brass was used.

A plating department comprising baths for gold, silver, copper, nickel, brass and solutions for various finishes.

I cannot tire you with all the things we did in metal, there are too many. This only serves to give you an idea of the numerous things made in our plant. I might add that the best workmanship and supervision in all our departments was of a high order. Quality came first at all times.

There were some failures, caused many times by trying to do the impossible but we learn through failure which often leads us to better things.

FAVRILE BRONZE GLASS AND ENAMEL BY LESLIE H. NASH

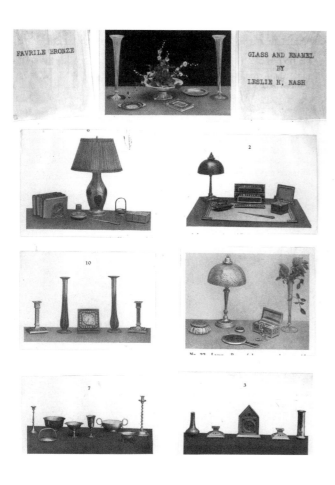

EXPORT

Our export trade was small and the pieces that were shipped overseas were not more than 2¹/₂ inches.[103] There were some about 4 in. tall that were mostly gold luster. The reason for this was the cost and duty. The prices ran from $5.00 each and up to $20.00 each. By the time they put their profit on and paid insurance and duty, it made the article too expensive for their trade. Business in Europe was always very slow. I don't think money was as plentiful as it is here in the United States.

There were a few buyers who bought very expensive pieces, but I rather imagine they were for collectors or museums. I think Germany was the most interested, France was second and England was very little. I am sure money was their problem.

When I think back it was amazing the quantity of our products that were sold in the United States and the

(LEFT) BRONZE ELEVATOR DOORS AND VITRIOUS ENAMEL ARCHECTURAL EXHIBITION CREATED FOR DALSTROM BY LESLIE H. NASH.

(RIGHT) INVENTION BY THE AUTHOR. THE ABOVE ELEVATOR DOOR WAS AN EXHIBITION PIECE FOR THE ARCHITECTURAL LEAGUE. IT IS MADE OF PERFORATED METAL INLAID WITH FAVRILE GLASS. DOOR FRAMES MADE BY THE DALSTROM METALIC DOOR COMPANY.

prices were never questioned. People like Marshall Field of Chicago, Shreve, Crump and Low of Boston, Caldwell of Philadelphia, Tiffany and Co. of New York were not cheap people and for merchandise of our standard they did a very large business for almost 40 years.

Dad always claimed that 40 years was the limit of any product and a drastic change must take place in order to go on.

FAVRILE POTTERY

An interesting process was used in the making of our pottery which is not apparent at a first glance.[101] Most of the designs were inspired from large blossoms and foliage. The designs were then executed in Repouse work in copper. A rather long process of development was required. The article so made was then molded into plaster-of-paris and allowed to dry in a warm room. Sections of the plaster mold were removed, reassembled, and tied together with string. The clay which was rather watery, was then poured into the, now dry, plaster mold, and allowed to remain until the plaster had absorbed a part of the water, thus causing the clay to adhere to the walls of the mold. When the desired thickness of clay was apparent, the residue was then poured out. The mold and the clay was then set aside to dry. The clay, upon drying, would shrink and thus permit easy withdrawal of the formed object. This clay formed object was then fired in a Kiln. Later, the glaze was sprayed on and then refired. After a careful cooling process, the finished object was removed. This method was used mostly on floral pieces.

Most pieces of Favrile Pottery were marked (L C T) The general color appearance of Favrile Pottery was a mixture of green and dull yellow: Occasionally a shade of deep blue.

(TOP) FAVRILE POTTERY PHOTOGRAPH FROM THE AUTHOR'S ALBUM.

(BOTTOM) FAVRILE POTTERY ALMOST ALL POTTERY WAS INSPIRED BY PLANTS AND BLOSSOMS. (MANY BEAUTIFUL PIECES MADE) PHOTOGRAPH FROM THE AUTHOR'S ALBUM.

THE TIFFANY FOUNDATION FOR ARTISTS

For some years Mr. Tiffany had spoken to me about his plans to establish the Tiffany Foundation for Artists. He seemed to be interested in my thoughts regarding the manner in which artists should be admitted to the Foundation. Perhaps it was because of my own association with an Art League on Long Island, that he felt I could advise him. I told him that I felt that interested students should personally make application to the Foundation, and be admitted by the regulations set up by the Trusties and on his own merit, rather than to be sent by the direction of various Art Leagues.

After some careful planning the Foundation was finally established in 1918 and Mr. Tiffany asked both my brother Douglas and myself to serve on the board of Trusties. My brother Douglas accepted in 1920, and served until September 1929 when he resigned. I was not able to accept due to my heavy burden at the factory. I think that Mr. Tiffany really wanted me to act more as an instructor, teaching the students in the many diversified creative things that we did at the factory.

I always felt that his offer was highly complimentary, but I just could not take on any more work.

As there has been a great deal written about the work of this Foundation, I shall not attempt to describe it in detail.

INSPIRATION

When I first started designing glass objects for the Tiffany Furnaces, I came to them with a fair amount of information on Art in general, but glass was a new problem, technically, chemically and a new medium to work with.

I discovered that I could get the most inspiration from my Father, Arthur J. Nash and Louis C. Tiffany. To me they were refreshing, both anxious to try new ideas. The expense, well that was never mentioned. The glass student and enthusiast would have no limit in his work with this quality of inspiration.

Our work never had to depend on the commercial side unduly. The determined effort to make something new and original, to excel and never to copy. Now and then a bit of the beauties of some forgotten periods may appear. It was always the aim of Mr. Tiffany and his coadjutors to be original.

In an art such as this; so closely covered by so many minds, it is not easy to succeed or even claim originality. However, this production shows skill, both in conception and execution and the work has gained favorable appreciation from the entire world.

THE GLASS HOUSE SYMPHONY

I have heard music all my life. As a young child I can remember giving up my play to stay indoors and listen to my Mother play the piano and sing. Mother was trained for the opera but to keep her voice well trained she sang light opera. She had a beautiful soprano voice and a wonderful range. I just adored to hear her sing. She was a Queenly type of person and beautiful to look at. I seem to be wandering, however, I was very sensitive to music.

One day as I sat in an old glassworkers chair, I noticed that in the glass house there are many combined sounds. There was the dull throbbing roar of the furnaces and Gloryholes, deep-throated vibrating, chains, the thump of the Presses, the sounds of the workers tools. The men calling to boy helpers would sing "Blow-Ho-Ho." Most of the men either sang or whistled. There was the hissing of steam and compressed air hoses, men and boys calling to others, the tinkle of glass, shoveling sounds, an occasional bell-like sound. All of this was covered with the golden light of the fires.

A loud telephone bell brought me back from my symphony into the daily grind of work. To see glass workers gathering, swinging, rolling, blowing, tooling, decorating and the movement that was all about. Oh! for those beautiful, wonderful days. This was truly a Symphony seldom found in other types of manufacture of today.

FLORENCE [102]

Florence by name was sent to see Dad about a job, by her family. She was very young but a little pressure was brought to bear so Dad tried to find a spot for her. She had very little education, however Dad put her in the showroom to keep the stock clean and neatly arranged. Everyone that ever came to the factory knew Florence and everyone thought the world of her.

Our office boys educated her trying to perhaps make a mail clerk or telephone switchboard operator out of her. She was always very attentive to Dad and would bring his lunch or tea in the afternoon.

Ed Meyran, our bookeeper was always trying to advance her job. He tried hard to get her to answer the phone. "Now, Florence," he would say, "I will go to an outside phone and give you a ring. When you hear me, say 'Hello, who is this?' You answer 'This is the Tiffany Furnaces. To Whom do you wish to speak?" Then Meyran would leave and call in. The answer in a high voice was always the same, "This is Florence."

Florence was a stock clerk for 20 years. We never could get her into a better job. She was happy and Dad gave her an advance every year. As long as I can remember she never wanted a thing that she didn't get. At Christmas every man in the plant saw to it that Florence had a happy Christmas. Everyone loved Florence. She loved the glass so much that she never wanted to leave the showroom.

When I look over my notes that remind me of these stories, it gives me a strange feeling. Its like a dream or *a* play that I saw years ago.

THE GLASS HAT
FIFTY MEN AND A GIRL

One Wednesday afternoon I was sent to meet a charming young dancer from Hollywood and her manager who drove to the glassworks in a Rolls-Royce with a chauffeur.[103]

Oh! yes, she was attractive with a slight accent which I could not place but which made her more interesting. Her manager was a stout and rather pompus man who did all the talking.

"You see, Mr. Nash, this young lady is making her debut in Hollywood and I am working on publicity for her. You, as a glass manufacturer, may be able to help us. The idea is this; first of all, I am sure you could make a ladies glass hat." I agreed that I could. "As you see the lady has long beautiful hair which touches the ground, she keeps it braided." She then let her hair fall to the floor.

"Now what we want is a hat made of vita glass which prevents the suns rays from changing the color of her hair. She will wear the hat at the Waldorf, drive in a Victoria through Central park, attend the theatre, walk down Fifth Avenue and in short create a mild sensation. Her picture will appear in the newspapers, the expense is no object." I quoted one thousand dollars for the job.

I began working on the glass. They were to telephone me the following Tuesday to tell me when they could come to the plant. All arrangements were made for Friday, the glass would be ready.

As was the custom in the glass factory most of the men, when working, wore no clothing above the belt. Going to them and telling them the story, I said that I thought it would look better if they put on their shirts as it showed a mark of respect for the lady.

Friday came and I was in the front office to greet my new friends. This was in July and it was hot and humid, the temperature in the factory was about 120° near the glass furnace. The girl's manager decided to stay in the office with his newspaper so the young lady and I went into the factory. Those glass workers were a sight, they had decided to put on a show and had put on everything, even sport jackets! However, they had provided a chair and a floor lamp for the girl. But I could at that time easily have thrown all of them into the furnace, I was so angry at them.

I told one of the men to take measurements and not to crush the lady's hair. He took the tape from me, went to the girl, touched her hair and ran away, much to the amusement of the other men. "Boss," he whispered, "I can't do it. It makes me shiver all over." I said in his ear, "You idiot, do as I say or get out."

These men were having a ball at my expense. I just could not stop them, all the other shops were watching the show, in fact, *all* work came to a standstill.

Finally, the measurements were taken with my help and the first hat was made, wide brim, dome shape crown. It was set aside to cool. In the meantime, I sent two men to bring a mirror from the showroom, "the small one," I said. Oh! no, they brought in the large one about 5 x 7 ft., full length. They leaned it against a post and smiled at me. Mind you, never had I seen them so polite. The humor of the situation was getting me and they knew it.

The hat was now ready. To get even with the man who balked at taking the measure of her head, I told him to put the hat on the girl. He said, "Boss, I can't do it, if I do, I shall die." With that remark the entire gang roared with laughter, including the dancer.

So I put it on, then the dancer went up to the mirror and danced in front of it pulling her skirt up just above the knee. She was so pleased and happy. The final hat was made and put in the oven to anneal. I said, "Men, the show is over," and escorted the dancer with a large twinkle in her eye, to the front office and her manager. They left and in a week they called for the hat, thanked me and drove off.

I have never to this day received the thousand dollars. The only thing I have to prove this story, is the picture that came out in a newspaper showing the hat on the girl.

GLASS HAT

FUTURE OF GLASS

If glass has lasted for 5000 years or more, I don't worry much about the future. I believe handmade glass will in a few years become rare. First because of the expense of fuel, chemicals, moulds, etc. and the labor costs have risen so high. The return is slow and the number of pieces of glass made becomes smaller and smaller. Union glass workers have made heavy demands on the manufacturer.

The future glass will be highly commercial in character. Pressed forms, mould blown, anything that will give a high rate of production. I think you will see the use of glass in building increase to a marked extent. Impregnated fine threads of glass used for boats is only an example of the sort of things you will see. Personally, I see a great future for glass in many fields.

I am conscious of the fact that plastics will take over some glass forms but I doubt very much that it will discourage glass manufacturing to any extent. As a container of liquids it will outlast any other material in the long run.

Glass tile has long been in my mind and only during the last few years has it made its place in architectural designs. There will develop many ways of using glass, not yet discovered. Therefore, I still hold promise of greater things to come in glass.

THE TIFFANY PLANT CLOSES FOREVER

It was before electric lighting was developed that candlesticks, oil lamps and gas lights provided the glass works with plenty of business, together with flat glass for windows, and colored glass for church windows and tableglass.

On a visit to England in 1906 I found many old glass works had closed and those that remained open were turning out electric light bulbs by the thousand. I am told they made very little profit. The automatic machines came in but only a few could afford them.

My father, therefor, was fortunate when he came to America in 1892 and was able to continue the manufacturing of his beautiful Art glass.

When the full impact of the depression hit us in 1929 and 1930, all business and building came to a full stop. We were a luxury business and the first to feel the shock. Retail sales fell to nothing. Contracts and estimating departments were laying off workers by the dozens. By the end of 1929 we were running into debt so fast that it would make our head spin. Mr. Tiffany and Dad were dumping money in to try and save the business but it was to no avail.

A Directors meeting was held and the Auditors read the statement which showed a heavy loss. It was voted to go into voluntary bankruptcy. Mr. Tiffany bought in all stock at Par, paid out all outstanding indebtedness and the famous glass business was closed forever. Shortly, thereafter, The Tiffany Studios with all it's departments did the same thing.

All this fell apart like a house of cards. This brought on my father's illness from which he never recovered. He passed on in his 86th year.[104] Mr. Tiffany had passed on a short time earlier. His son Charles L. died and then my brother Douglas. W. H. Thomas had died some years before.

This leaves me the only survivor to tell the story of Favrile glass and correct the many erroneous statements made about our glass and it's art and manufacture.

I have been asked to write this story, not only by my family, but by many others who collect and sell "Favrile" products.

"ANGEL" A FAVRILE GLASS MOSAIC
DESIGNED BY ARTHUR J. NASH
AUTHOR'S COLLECTION

THE TIFFANY FURNACES, INC.

SHOPS AND DEPARTMENTS

It may prove interesting to mention the set up of our Factory:

Batch mixing rooms

Labratory

Six shops of glass makers

Flat glass for church windows and Mosaics

Modeling Shop

Pottery, two kilns, moulding department

Foundry for small casting—later dispensed with

Enameling Department—kilns, etc.

Art Department

Five showrooms

Photographic Department

Plating and Finishing Department

Polishing and Grinding

Shipping and Packing rooms

Engine room—Boilers

Assembling Department

Audit Office

General Offices—bookkeeping

Estimating Department

Pattern room

Carpenters shop

Mold room

Etching Department

Flat glass stockrooms

Fire house and equipment

First aid room

Cutting and Polishing shop

DEPARTMENTS

Private Offices:

Arthur J. Nash	Vice President
A. Douglas Nash	Secretary and Treasurer
Leslie H. Nash	Production Manager

Studio and Experimental room

Metal Departments:

    Lamps

    Desk sets

    Boxes

    Frames

    Lighting Fixtures

    Elevator and bank doors

    Lighting glass

    Globes

    Shades and pendant fixtures

Metal Show Room:

    Lamps

    Enamels

Art cutting shops

Lathes and spinning

Twelve thousand gallons oil storage

Chemicals in bulk storage

Coke and soft coal storage

Pot storage and pot arch

Glass mold shop and storage

Kitchen

Engraving shop

Seven stockrooms

One main showroom

Enamel Department

Packing and shipping

Metal Show room

FAVRILE CRAFTSMAN AT WORK IN A
CORNER OF THE METAL SHOP

General Offices

Boiler and Engine Room.

Machine Shop—machines for every purpose.

KINDS OF FAVRILE GLASS

(Listed by colors)

Gold Luster	Ascot Red	Yellow
Blue Luster	Flint Crystal	Celadon
Green Luster	Moonstone	Pomona Green
Shell Pink	Florescent	Grotto Blue
Apple Green	Avonturine green	Cinnavar Blue
Mazarine Blue	Yellow and Opal	
Ruby	Golden Yellow	
Samian Red	Opaque Yellow	
Venetian Red	Foliage	
Purple Violet	Drapery	
Blue Violet	Opal	
Blue Violet and Opal	Pink	
Opalescent Blue and Violet	Blue	
Opal Green and Red	Black	
Onyx	Gray	
Larva	Purple	
Heavenly Blue	Lt. Green	

(Other Kinds of Favrile)

Reticulated	Reactive	Carved Rock Crystal
Satin (Acid Dip)	Cameo	Tinted Cut glass
Laminated	Etched	Devitrified
Aquamarine		

WINDOW GLASS—was made in hundreds of varying colors. A large stock was always carried.

Pressed jewels

Chipped jewels

Scarabs—Luster, large and small.

Tiles—4 × 4 Luster various (designs inspired by chineese sword guards).

Tiles—1 × 1 Luster

Tiles—2 × 2 Luster

Tiles—6 × 6 various

Many various Jewel shapes—Cabashone jewels, Emerald—chipped-Ruby. Jewels and others

Turtle backs—Luster

Pressed glass was given little attention at our plant and was seldom used.

Lighting glass was a large part of our manufacture. Dome shades in many patterns, globes, pendants, prisms, glass for leaded shades and church window glass.

This is only a partial list of the many kinds of glass Favrile glass.

THE LAST PAGE[105]

You must realize by this time that I feel that an injustice has been done. Anyone can understand that a man with a wife and six children cannot exist very long on nothing. A baby girl died before coming to the United States and a few months after arriving a four year old son died of smoke poisoning when someone who hated the English tried to burn his new home.[106] His three sons were surrounded after leaving Church and beaten with staves. Also to add to this man's suffering the factory just completed was burned to the ground wiping out his entire investment and then realizing that the refinancing of the

Company brought about a condition where he lost control from a partnership to a man who gained control by a small margin.

I have been asked many times why this man did not assert himself under the circumstances. A man's first thought is for his family and during the time when the business was being established, things were hard for this man. He was taken advantage of in many ways but he knew that he dare not take any liberties until his home and family were established. In a short time this man had proved his ability in his business and things were developing at a fast pace but the damage had been done.

It was when I reviewed these painful circumstances that I decided to write this story and bring a man, a deserving man, out into the light. No man who has contributed something worthy to his country should be ignored. This man was my late Father, Arthur J. Nash, vice president of the Louis C. Tiffany Furnaces, Inc., makers of FAVRILE glass. A glass chemist of unquestioned ability in the production of Art glass in both England and America with many awards to his credit.[107]

THE ALBUM OF EARLY GLASS

One of the greatest surprises from the Nash archives is a small album with more than sixty photographs of early Tiffany glass. Until now, no contemporary photographs of the vessels made during the first years of Tiffany's production were known—or even suspected—to exist. The earliest pictorial records that we had of Tiffany's endeavors in this medium had been a group photograph of six objects that appeared in an advertisement for Favrile glass in the February 1896 issue of the *Art Interchange*. Additional photographs appeared in 1896 in a small promotional brochure, *Tiffany Favrile Glass*. Thereafter, the company issued photographs of its vases on a steady basis, and these were then used by the many magazines that featured laudatory articles about Tiffany's achievements. While these later images and the later glassware are familiar, the photographs in Nash's book are exceptional and lead us into terra incognita.

This is not to say that Tiffany's first essays in glass production were totally unknown. In fact, they have been the object of recent research.[108] Nonetheless, they are at quite a remove from the elegant shapes and suave iridescence of Tiffany's later glass—from the years around 1900 and thereafter. These early works embody a far different and bolder language of form. There is a youthful, experimental vigor. The molten glass was pushed and squeezed into unheard-of and even disproportionate forms. Paddled, dimpled, deflated, their shapes are in every way the antithesis of the symmetry traditionally associated with glassblowing. If one

did not know they had been produced in the early 1890s, one might well believe they had been made after 1960 under the influence of Peter Voulkos and Harvey Littleton's expressionist forms. Likewise, the bold veining of the glass—the colored filaments pulled, swirled, and feathered—is quite distinctive. Although some of the glass is lustered or iridescent, and Nash has identified these works, most are mat; some of the surfaces are exceptionally dry and stonelike because they have been treated with acid.

When production began, the finished pieces were marked with long, thin paper labels that proclaimed "TIFFANY FABRILE GLASS" (see the vase illustrated on p. 193). This trade name, supposedly conceived by Arthur J. Nash, was derived from the Latin *fabrilis*, meaning "of an artisan, or craftsmanlike."[109] By 1893, the labels bore the trade name *Favrile*, a word with a more French resonance. Tiffany, through the pen of Charles de Kay, glossed over the change, claiming it was "a name easily spoken . . . the root being *faber*."[110] In addition, there was a second paper label, one that bore the registration number of the particular object, and it is these numbered labels that we see displayed in front of many of the vases in the photos. By about vase 6000, this system was changed to one in which the registration number was engraved directly into the underside of the vase.

Production of Favrile glass reputedly began in late 1892, and by late 1894 it was being advertised and sold in New York City. Much of it was thus dispersed to individual clients. A large group was bought by Tiffany's great patron Henry O. Havemeyer, and presented to The Metropolitan Museum of Art. Tiffany, ever conscious of the value of publicity, also sent a substantial gift to the emperor of Japan, and it is now preserved in the Imperial Museum of Tokyo. Another large collection was designated for the Smithsonian Institution in Washington, and yet a fourth group was bought by the Cincinnati Museum of Art. The glass was sold in Europe by S. Bing and his L'Art Nouveau gallery in Paris; via this route, many works entered the collections of Europe's leading museums of decorative arts. Lastly, as he did throughout his career, Tiffany kept certain specimens for himself. The initials *LCT* are penned under several of the photographed examples, but Tiffany evidently kept others as well.[111] The distinctively asymmetrical gourd, which appears on page 35 of the album, can be identified as a vase that he kept for his collection and selected to illustrate in *The Art Work of Louis C. Tiffany*. Also, Arthur J. Nash put aside examples for his own collection, including the very first two works blown at the Corona plant, and many of these are identified in the Nash photos.[112]

Because this early glass is so distinctive and no two pieces are exactly alike, many of the works photographed in Nash's album can be identified with extant objects (see the vases on pp. 193–203). Others were bought in New York by representatives of the Berlin Kunstgewerbemuseum in 1893. Many are works that have come down to us through the museum collections that were formed in the mid-1890s. Also, several of the photographed vases correspond to ones from the important collections of early Tiffany glass formed by the late James H. Stubblebine and by Eric Streiner. The correlation of photographs and extant objects is very instructive. In certain instances, it allows us to confirm the attribution of these otherwise atypical pieces to Tiffany's factory. In some cases, it allows us to reestablish the original Tiffany registration number, and this, in turn, will help to chart a more precise chronology of this period of experimental glassblowing.

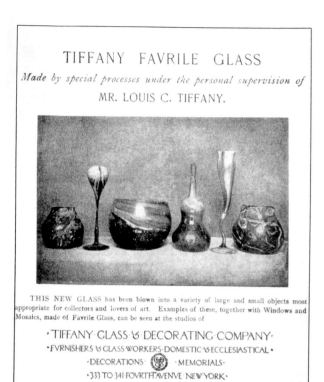

TIFFANY GLASS & DECORATING COMPANY ADVERTISEMENT FROM *ART INTERCHANGE*, FEBRUARY 1896.

The origins of Nash's album are not readily apparent. The actual book is merely a commercial ledger with lined, numbered pages. It was perhaps an old book that was on hand; significantly, the first twenty-six pages were removed, perhaps because they had previously been used for other purposes. Clearly, the mounting of the photographs is not official or even professional; it is a casual, homemade affair.

Although the handwritten title page proclaims "Tiffany Favrile Glass Compiled by Leslie H. Nash," the evidence indicates that the photographs had been made a decade before Leslie joined the firm. The handwritten title page also proclaims "Tiffany Furnaces Inc.," which is an inexact corporate name. The company name of "Tiffany Furnaces," instituted in 1902, was changed in January 1920 to "Louis C. Tiffany Furnaces, Inc." and was retained until the company was dissolved in April 1924. It is undoubtedly the latter corporation name that Nash has abridged, but the album seems to have been composed even after that firm terminated. Indeed, on line 6 he refers to himself as "Designer and Production Mgr for 24 years," which is a claim he could not have made until 1933. This gives us a *terminus post quem* for the album and may help to explain how it came to be. In the wake of the great stock-market crash of 1929, the ensuing bankruptcy, the demise of Tiffany's empire, the dispersal of stock, and the closing of the offices, Leslie Nash apparently gathered up old documentary material left behind. The old photographs and the commercial copybook were used ad hoc to make a photo album. Because the annotations are in different inks, we can presume that they were written at various points in time—although it is not clear if this was in the 1930s or, more probably, in the 1940s and 1950s.

There is a curious gap in the pagination between pages 48 and 55. It is possible that these pages were already missing from the book when Nash decided to convert it to a photograph album, or perhaps there were previously used pages that he himself removed. It is equally possible that these pages once contained photographs that Leslie Nash took out in the 1950s. Indeed, he used a photograph of early glass that must have once been in this album for his manuscript *Tiffany Favrile Glass*.[113] One can only speculate, then, whether more photographs of early glass have been lost.

As is evident, these photographs were not carefully composed and executed in the studio of a professional photographer. Everything points to their having been made in an offhand manner, probably within the factory's storage room. While care may have been taken in some of the arrangements, many of the compositions seem awkward. The overall lighting is poor and not artistic. Certainly, the backdrops are provisional: the paper is often wrinkled, and there are visible seams. Most telling of all, many of the vases are accompanied by paper labels with their respective registration num-

bers. In short, the photographs appear to have been taken only as *aides-mémoires* meant for internal use within Tiffany Studios.

When were the photographs made? Even though Nash penned the dates of 1898, 1904, 1906, 1910, and even 1912 on some of them, these cannot be correct for either the vessels or the photographs.[114] Nor are his errors surprising; he not uncommonly assigned incorrect years. These photographs must have been made somewhat earlier, and there are several different ways this can be determined. First, the subject of these photographs—the earliest of Tiffany's glass—helps date the images. The extraordinarily free forms of the glass relates exclusively to the wares produced in the very first years of glassmaking, which would mean from late 1892 to 1893. It is significant that none of the characteristic types of Tiffany glass from 1895 to 1900 are evident. There is no Cypriote glass with visible pitting of the surface, no vessels with peacock feathers, and none with millefiore technique.

The earliness of these photographs can be established in other ways as well. The photograph on page 36 of the album is the same one used by Tiffany Studios in the advertisement in the February 1896 issue of the *Art Interchange*. It is not merely that the two images are of the same objects arranged in the same order, but, rather, there is an exact correspondence in key areas. If we compare the bowls at the far sides (both of which are in The Metropolitan Museum of Art—see page 194), the two bowls have been positioned exactly the same, and their striations of colored glass are exactly the same. The inescapable conclusion is that both images were derived from a single negative. The print used for the advertisement was evidently touched up for its new purpose: the paper labels with the registration numbers were covered over, as were the horizon line and the seam in the background. None of this retouching is visible in the advertisement, but its image is not only small, but also gray and grainy.

Because time has to be allowed for the photograph to

have been processed and the advertisement prepared, we can conclude that the photograph must have been taken no later than the end of 1895. This *terminus ante quem* corresponds to the general date of the objects pictured in the album. We can also conclude that the photographs were ordered by Arthur Nash or Louis C. Tiffany, even if we do not yet know exactly why they were taken. By 1900, when the next phase of Favrile glass was in production, these photographs would undoubtedly have seemed out of date and even useless. One can well imagine that they were cast to the side, which would also explain why some of them faded and deteriorated. Still later, they may have been found lying about by Leslie Nash, or perhaps his father intentionally handed over these historic mementos. In any event, it is to Leslie's credit that he thought to gather them up and preserve them in this makeshift album.

Thus far, we have emphasized the pictorial element in the album, but Leslie Nash's textual glosses are also significant. Some of them are fairly generic; certain claims are deceptive. For instance, on page 48 of the album, he rightly noted that the metal mounts for the vases were made at Tiffany Studios but misleadingly added a note claiming that he set up the metal department. Even if Nash's notes sometimes constitute a minefield, there are positive contributions that cannot be overlooked. Of great significance, for example, is his explanation on page 37 of the letter code that Tiffany Furnaces used as a pricing system. His description on page 76 of Diamond Jim Brady as a customer is charming. His remarks on page 96 about Arthur Nash's experiments in luster glass are informative. Not least of all, on the last page, there is a brief but precious history of the Nash family.

In short, this album is an extremely important document. When interpreted carefully, it constitutes a major contribution to our understanding of Tiffany's glass-making.

Tiffany Furnaces Inc,
Corona L.I. N.Y.

—"—

Tiffany Favrile Glass
Compiled by
Leslie H. Nash

Designer and Production Mgr for 24 years
covering the period
of blown glass to about 1915

The Company started to make glass
the latter part 1892 or early 98 — 1893 Sept   1892 Oct

property of   L. H. Nash

Dates are not
quite right. I do not
find the exact dates
but the latter part
of 1892 the factory
was building.
actual glass making
started about Sept
or Oct 1893 —

These photographs were taken from the
early collection kept as a record in a special room   by L H Nash

The glass in this book

is early Favrile glass —
made from 1895 To about 1912 — possibly a little later 1914
a J Nash was afraid to use
luster glass because he was
afraid it would look cheap in
large quantity — so he only used it
for decoration — in the last few
pages — however the demand
was insistant, and when it
hit the market it was like a
gold rush — you couldent stop it —

I just love the early glass shown
here — most of the forms are
are highly creative — and designed
by Dad — The prices were not high
I only wish these photographs were
in color —

L H Nash
Production Mgr

LCT   25"   5"   15"

11   10"   18"   LCT   20"

20ʺ   14ʺ   lamp globe   8ʺ

All prices of Favrile Glass — were established
not on production records but on
artistic merit — alone.

The numbers on the small tags
do not tell the age of the piece — they are
applied only when shipment is made.

numbering started from #1 to 10000
then A1 — A2 up to A10000 then B1 — B2 est
to A10000 and so on — then 1A — 2A est to 10000

Iridescence was not much used at this time
but later the public demanded it.

18"   25"   20"   10"   15"

All glass was marked

LCT   L.C. Tiffany   L.C. Tiffany Favrile

Favrile -   Ex Louis C. Tiffany or Exhibition
sometimes the place - as Paris Ex Louis C Tiffany Favrile
all of the above bore a number -
        with the exception of table glass ware,
such as wine glasses and small articles
large fruit bowls will have a number
also Comports - will bare a letter which
represents a certain decoration -
Small lighting glass - globes ect (Favrile)

L. M. Nash
Designer + Production mgr.

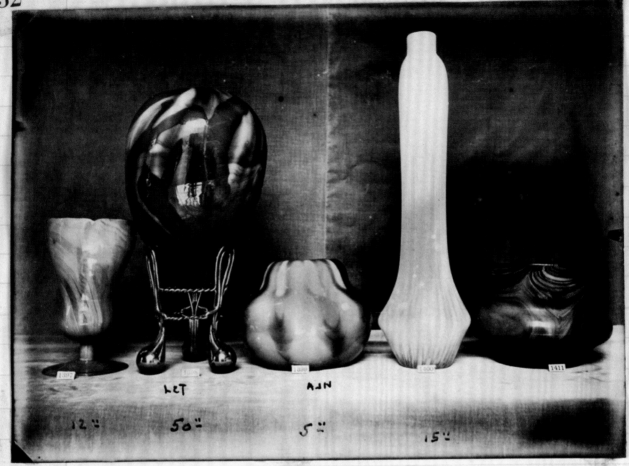

LCT   AJN

12"   50"   5"   15"

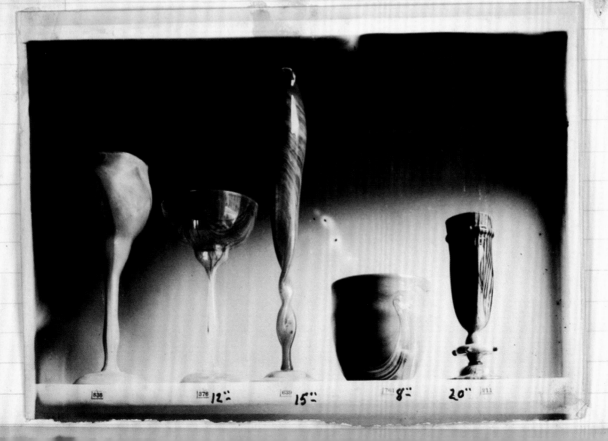

12"   15"   8"   20"

Most of the pieces in this book were designed
on a blackboard in the factory by Arthur J Nash
and Louis C Tiffany — Glass entirely by a Jnash

Early 15" to 20"

LCT

Very Early 15" to 20"

1900

Some pieces were licked about the floor.
This was LCT's idea & being original – See 1228

£30⁵ to 40⁵
Early
Gonard~

tear bottle

At two different times they further thinned
to leave and sell out, if this rule was broken.

No glass was ever put into a furnace except by A J Nash
woNaish or Leslie H Nash.

1904   18″ to 40″   Texture effects - all HJN

20″   18″   LCT   30″   AJN   20″

middle period -
a little more formal

L.C. Tiffany had some ideas, but
they were impractical - some were made
but the sales were few.

Almost all the early designs
were made by Arthur J Nash
all colors and effects were
were made by him from his own formula
M⁰ Nash never permitted any other
person to prepare glass - until
my brother Douglas and myself entered the business.
Iridescent glass was invented by a Nash
and used later - he had made it in England

I shall mark the prices where ever I can
but there will be no piece less than $5 ⁰⁰ very few at this price
The prices shown are retail.

The price code - GAINWEMUST
      1 2 3 4 5 6 7 8 9 0
This may be of use later on to
collectors - some pieces still have
a sticker with these letters on as GW^TT = 15 ⁰⁰
W - TT = 5 ⁰⁰ NW^Th/4 5 ⁰⁰ etc

Early dip mould

Gourard type

30"   20"   30"

A J N

Down thro' the ages the decoration by use
of a thread - comes once more to Favrile Glass

821 8"   545 40"   199 30"   10" 700   10" 661

500 15"   215 12"   299 20"   10" 13   ACT 40"
                                          not for glass

1906

620   552   510   658

708   514   518 $40··

Composition of these forms the
as in other art is to get away from conventional

First luster glass
put on the market.

60⁻ ⁻ACT 40⁻ 15⁻

"50⁻ 30⁻ 30⁻ 40⁻

about 12 to $ 60⁻

25⁻ 50⁻ 55" 40⁻ 20⁻ 3ch⁻

In 1909 All glass was increased 50%
and a year later the more important   ✳
ones to an increase of 100%.

1906   H.O. Havemeyer   called at factory
to see some of the new pieces, he is
making a fine collection.

The effort of all those who had anything to do
with design, was to be original - and to avoid
if possible copying any form ever made in glass
and I may say that is a big order.

The color and chemical treatment also was used
in an original manner.

18" 10⁻

40" 20" 10" 5" 15" 18"

all A.W.

20⁻ 15⁻

15" 8"

1908

Vari colored pieces –

a study of early glass by L.H. Nash

There is a grandeur about the work of a J.M— the pieces I have collected, designed by L.C.T. show very little skill in Glass art. A.J.N tells me – that L.C.T tried to overload Cu in the glass and everything blew bob sided or cracked to bits.

I note that L.C Tiffany has no knowledge of glass chemistry and that A.J.N later told me if any one tried to put glass mixtures into the furnaces, he would shut the place up –

It was to be A.J.N & A.D.N and L.H.N and no one else –

This I found out later when I was doing the glass filling for A.J.N – and received my instructions as above –

Gold Luster
iridescent
30"

The metal mounted pieces were done at the Tiffany Studios factory of course.
Our metal department started some later –

25" 26" 15 ½"

compact thread.

20" 18" 10" 10"

60" 20"

12"

14" 12" 20" 10"

56 - 1910

10" to 20"
increased from 30 to 75"

Most of the early pieces were opaque - in browns -
Green - blue - yellow mixed effects. Opal
and flint were also used -

The next ten or twelve pages - show
a somewhat different glass, more
formal in design - and translucent
1910

Few pieces made up to this time were
of utilitarian design - but there
are many pieces which can be used
for flowers -

Sales were somewhat slow until a change was made
art in glass was not understood to any extent

$ 10 to 20

With new forms - more stable in design not so heavy - are doing well
all sales increased from 12 1/2 % to
131 %

beautiful form and color

12"   18"   15"   40"   pale blue
20"

18"   10"   15   5"

mad about 1912

Color plays most important part from most on 1900

LCT bad

#112 never was any good
If LCT has his way. wod put things on a stem of barley

These early forms designed by W Nash made Sales jump - art of flint

Clear glass forms come into being 1900

Flint glass continued

good threads

from 50 to 100.00 en

A more useful type. beautiful color

1912 lustre introduced again

At this time A Nash introduced a little gold glass as a decoration
the sales then increased to three times the previous year.

Early glass did not sell very fast
Designs become more formal.

This about ends the opaque type of glass about 1898
Clear forms with delicate lustre appear introduced by
Cypresses

from 1903 prices were advanced thirty
3 times higher
The sales of the lighter glass was so rapid, we could
not make it fast enough — prices were increased 100%.

Sales pick up. more delicate glass was used
with pure colors

See our
collection

Diamond Jim Brady - is very much
impressed with our glass - and gives all
his Christmas presents of it - bought at
Tiffany & Co -
He would come into Tiffany & Co -
and drop his card into the pieces
he liked - giving a list of names
and addresses - to Mr Arthur & Rose
then in charge of China & Glass at T.

'57

The passing year brought more refinement
of form — it made more money, but I hated it.
RAB

"Mrs Russel Sage has become one of our customers"

Russel Sage starts collection
See Memorial window Far Rockaway L I N.Y.
given in memorial by Mrs R Sage

Gold lustre first made its impression
at the Paris Exhibition of 1900 - while Arthur J Nash
had made much of this glass in England
it was (Copper + Silver) lustre - this was
recognized by the French jury - for which he
received a special award.

It is interesting to note here that having
personally been responsible for perfecting
iridescent effects - and having invented peacock
green lustre - and reproduced the Egyptian
lustre effects - which by the way no one but myself
could do. I made only about 60 pieces.
and each piece was sold in a velvet case
the prices being 50⁰⁰ up to 300⁰⁰

but in checking back over my fathers books
on lustre glass made in England I discovered the same
formula that we have used for all Favrile
lustre glass - there have been a few minor
changes made by my brother Douglas and myself -

It is strange indeed to find almost every
writer giving the entire credit for lustre glass
to Louis C Tiffany - may I at this time correct these
people - having worked with Mr Tiffany for twenty
three years - he never contributed one thing
to the chemical part of lustre glass - and when I
made a change I never gave the information
to a living soul - and my personal record just
show many changes in its production.

To be original in glass form
was very difficult — 3000 years
of glass manufacture to cope with. Offers a
problem

Opalescent effects decorated with green
and gold, created a sensation.

Some given sent to Paris Exhibition 1900
first award

60ᵒᵒ up

Clean pure lines, simple form
have great charm.

We had many requests for pure
white milk glass – but none of us
felt that there was real artistic merit
in this cold color – very few pieces will be
found –

20ᵒᵒ to 35ᵒᵒ

#477 the famous lilly form. thousands of these
pieces were sold
every year.

Did now uses his lustre effects.
Sales bonus.

6 to 14" many sizes m.

In 1897 Arthur J. Nash introduced luster glass based on experiments that he had been working on for many years before coming to this country (America) as his books show. he had perfected a copper luster and a silver mirror luster as his formulas show - (Experimental piece in my collection -)

And checking my own formula which I used at the Tiffany factory with his early formula, I discovered that it was basicly the same (B²) glass, I also noted that a formula was made later F² glass which was not used extensively - then B' glass came in which my brother Douglas tried to get a fine gold. (failed) So A.J.n. told me to carry on some work for him. which put us back to B². the original which I used later and perfected. to gain the finest luster the world has ever known -

and later I invented peacock Emerald green luster. which for brillience surpassed all others -

see piece in my collection 3 legs.
Spider web or luster / luster / Eng Luster / silver   [signature] D.H.Nash

It was at this time, I made many changes in the treatments two inventions that I contributed - produced many remarkable effects - Emerald green - Sun burst tints and Green blue effects - this made possible the reproduction of the colors found in early Egyptian and glass found at Cyprus

Metal - & enamel - designed by Leslie H. Nash and produced entirely by him - profit in this department outstanding - it was at the close of the plant. the most profitable of all departments - that was the reason I went into that type of business later on - (L. H. Nash Metal Arts)

Here are a few pictures of the product of Tiffany Favrile metal & enamel.

This does not include jewelry - which was made at Tiffany & Co - for L C T. The purchase of the enamel department and its transfer of personnel was the start of enamel work at our factory. We did not manufacture jewelry - but used it in lamps, desk sets, clocks, and many other objects. I took a personal interest in this work and developed the large bronze & enamel doors which you will see among my pictures. this was big business. Banks, elevator doors, lighting fixtures ect which went into five figures. and was wonderful until all important building came to a sudden stop about 1928 to 31 -

Many contracts exceeded $75,000 = which was a large sum for our type of work. The doors were enamel - inlaid glass in enamel metal, brushed steel - & bronze some doors perforated etched designs backed up with luster glass -

Two pairs of doors created a sensation at the Architectural Exhibition at the Grand Central Palace - which resulted in some fabulous sales over $160,000 = in orders resulted

for Stories - see other papers -
   The torn pongee suit of L C T
   The glass hat - (Martha Lorber) - dancer
   Song - Countess of Lonsdale - English story
   Steak & beer - overtime -
   Old John Hollingsworth -
   Flip flops & Jacobs ladders -
   Blowing on the punty - (Blow)
   Kee to the Pot Arsh - new boys
   4 foot bubbles - (Kunze)
   Pot Setting -
   Paper weights - (lunch hour)
   A bit O glass for the old woman
   The glass parade
   Baby cups
   Glass dress Paris 88 Ex Spun glass
   Mexican Curtains - mosaic
   Curtis Pub mosaic (Maxfield Parrish)
   The Bathers - Tiffany Window at Oysterbay
   The Chancel - St John the divine now at Oysterbay
   Whispering in Show Room - 23st

Born at Orset House Starbridge Eng -
Mother Fannie St Clare Taylor -
Father Arthur J. Nash my grandfather
Uncles of arm - matthew mark, luke, john, Jesse Nash
Cousin Fred Nash. Nash the great Architect of Eng -
Shakespeare's grand daughter married a Nash of our family
Name - Attenash (original) finally Nash - Stoke on Trent
The Nash family came to America in 1892
Fannie St Clare Taylor Nash Arthur John Nash
Percival Brett, Arthur Douglas, Leslie Hayden, Gerald
Lawrence Watson, and Norman, who died that same
year - first location Brooklyn - for about
one year - then to Flushing, a short time in
Corona L.I. while Factory was being built then
finally back to Flushing L.I. N.Y.
   Arthur J. Nash bought part of 90 acres.
mark Twain estate at Redding Conn
remodeled house built lake planted
trees - and made a beautiful garden -
   The entire place was a picture

Pressing glass

THE POTTERY ALBUMS

Another exciting surprise from the Nash archives is two slim, oblong albums with photographs of Tiffany pottery and some glass. Unlike the album with photographs of early glass, which seems to have been put together by Leslie Nash in the 1930s, these two were prepared in Tiffany's studio at a fairly early date, around 1905. Perhaps they were intended for use in the showroom or for distribution to salesmen and retailers.

Although they are not identical (they have different covers), they are both commercially made albums of similar dimensions intended to hold photographs and, most important, their contents are quite similar. The principal photographs are horizontal in format (and thus in accord with the format of the albums) and are professionally arranged compositions containing from two to five objects. The set of photographs in one album is quite similar to that in the other; perhaps the two sets were originally identical, but some pages may have been removed. In one album Leslie Nash (or perhaps someone else) has penned in the letters *A*, *B*, *C*, etc., under the objects in each photo. In the second album, Nash marked an *X* under those vases that, he writes, won "many awards"—probably referring to the fact that these models were displayed at various exhibitions. Since the photographs in both albums have in varying degrees been degraded by exposure to light, we have chosen to use the best surviving print where there are duplicates, irrespective of which album it came from.

In addition, one of the albums has a number of supple-mentary photographs that were not part of the main sequence but are nonetheless contemporary. Not only are they of a different format—single vases rather than group compositions—but they are also vertical compositions. Moreover, the most distinguishing characteristic of these ceramic vases is their bronze mountings. Both albums also include a small number of photos of glass vases.

The origins of the pottery department can be quickly retold.[115] In 1900, when Tiffany returned from the World's Fair, a reporter from Adelaide Alsop Robineau's New York–based magazine *Keramic Studio* reported that Tiffany had been intrigued by the forms and glazes of the French ceramics that he had just seen in Paris, so much so that he intended to try his hand in this medium. Indeed, he began experimenting before the end of 1900, and it was probably around then that he set up the pottery studio in his Corona plant.[116] At the same time, he made arrangements to borrow or buy a selection of these French wares from S. Bing, owner of L'Art Nouveau gallery in Paris, and also his European representative. Tiffany opened an exhibition of these French ceramics at his New York store in 1901. Ever conscious of the publicity value of exhibitions and prizes, Tiffany exhibited some of his first pottery in April 1904 at the St. Louis World's Fair and again, a year later, at an exhibition staged by the New York Keramic Arts Society. In September 1905, in conjunction with the opening of Tiffany & Co.'s new building at Fifth Avenue and 37th Street, the ceramic wares were exhibited en masse and officially put on the market.[117] Many of the first designs—elaborately sculpted models with vegetal shapes—were cast from vessels that had first been created in the enamel department. There were two principal glazes: the first to be introduced was likened to old ivory because it ranged from a transparent light yellow to black, and then a mossy green was introduced.

After a brief initial flurry of interest among journalists, little was heard about this department's products—although the same could be said about most of Tiffany's work from this period forward. Some pottery was exhibited at the 1905 exhibition of the New York Keramic Arts Society and at other small exhibitions. Examples of the pottery were included in his display at the Paris Salon in 1906, but for the most part, there was little coverage.[118] Because we know of a good number of ceramics with deep turquoise glaze—a color not mentioned in the earliest publicity—and others with brown, red, and other glazes, it is possible that these were later innovations.

The only other later development that can be documented concerns the combination of metals with the pottery. Tiffany probably first began mounting glazed but otherwise unornamented ceramic forms with bronze cages of floral decoration. Three of these are photographed in Nash's album. Tiffany Furnaces then began producing ceramics whose exteriors were bronze-coated. By 1908, the firm had developed a line of bronzed ceramic lamp bases and blown glass shades with matching electrodeposit decoration.[119] Tradition has it that although the pottery was not particularly successful, production continued on for a number of years until it ceased before 1920.

This brief history of the pottery department is a useful guide against which to read Leslie Nash's account. His text appears on a page added at the front of one of the photograph albums, and although it is presented as a straightforward history, it is misleading.

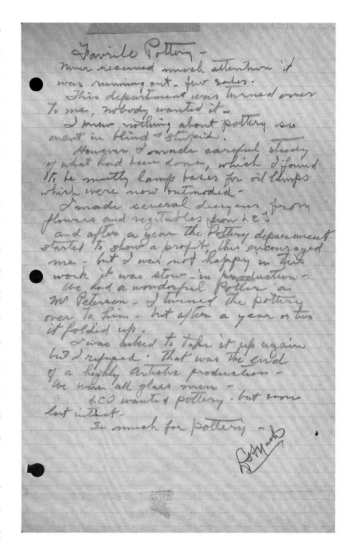

PAGE INSERTED AT THE FRONT OF ONE OF THE POTTERY ALBUMS

Favrile Pottery—

Never received much attention[.] it was running out—few sales.

This department was turned over to me, nobody wanted it—

I knew nothing about pottery so went in blind & stupid.

However I made careful study of what had been done, which I found to be mostly lamp bases for oil lamps which were outmoded—

I made several designs from flowers and vegetables from LCT and after a year the pottery department started to show a profit, this encouraged me—but I was not happy in this work[.] it was slow—in production—We had a wonderful Potter a Mr Petersen—I turned the pottery over to him—but after a year or two it folded up.

I was asked to take it up again but I refused. That was the end of highly artistic production— We were all glass men—

LCT wanted pottery—but soon lost interest— So much for pottery—

LH NASH

How are we to interpret Nash's words? First, his history omits the early portion of the pottery's existence, from its inception until about 1909 when Nash came to Tiffany. This is probably due not to his presumption that we knew this early stage but, rather, that he did not know it himself. Moreover, it had been a department in which his father had evidently not been involved. On the other hand, the history he describes and that he knew personally—the period after 1909—is quite interesting. He reminds us that a significant portion of the ceramic production was devoted to making bases for fuel lamps. Some of the models designated for that purpose are noted on the photographs, and indeed, a substantial number of vessels mounted as lamps are known. Nash's text suggests that new designs continued to be introduced in the second decade of the century. Also, he confirms previously heard rumors that the pottery department had been unprofitable. Yet, his is a more nuanced and undoubtedly correct history of the pottery's fortune—namely, that it had gone into an unprofitable decline before his arrival, was momentarily resuscitated under his direction, and then sank back down. On one of the photographs, he indicated that ceramics were produced until 1917, but elsewhere in his notes, he wrote that the pottery department closed in 1919. Even if the exact date cannot be fixed with precision, the general sense of his chronology agrees with what had previously been concluded.[120] Thus, as brief as his account is, it sheds new light on this aspect of Tiffany's work.

Whereas Nash's textual portion was evidently written well after the event, the albums and the photographs themselves are substantially older. The earliest known use of the photographs is as illustrations for an article that appeared in January 1906 in *Dekorative Kunst*.[121] This article included two group photographs of the pottery. One is a photograph that appears in both pottery albums (page 181, bottom). The second is of another group photograph, but curiously it no longer appears in either album; on the other hand, it probably once was included because Nash used it to accompany his own manuscript (see page 122). As we have already seen with the photographs of early glass, he occasionally removed photographs when he needed them for his own purposes. Other photographs from this series were used for the March 1906 issue of *International Studio*.[122] In regard to the two photographs that appeared in the January issue of *Dekorative Kunst*, because sufficient time must be allowed for the photos to have been obtained in New York and sent to Germany, it can be concluded that Tiffany Furnaces must have photographed their new ceramic vases by mid- or late 1905. This date, fittingly enough, corresponds to the moment in September 1905 when the pottery was officially put on the market and exhibited at the opening of Tiffany & Co.'s new store.

A much later dating might have been suggested by the substantially later dates that Nash annotated on some of the photos. On one, he wrote, "Pottery—1912 not made after 1917," and another proclaims, "A collection of Pottery and glass made at the Tiffany Furnaces Corona L.I. 1925." But these dates should not be taken literally, since Nash frequently added dates that he thought were appropriate but that often prove wrong.

At the lower left corner of one set of photographs (the set with the designations A to E), there are negative numbers composed of a primary series designation (6128) and then a separate suffix for each negative.[123] They demonstrate a basic sequence, running from 6128-1 to 6128-13, save that two are missing. But there are eight other images, all unnumbered, that cannot be fit within this sequence. Also, there is a previously mentioned photograph that appeared in *Dekorative Kunst*. These nine images cannot be assigned numbers in direct continuation of the series because such numbers (6128-14 to 6128-17) were used for photographs of glass. On the other hand, the subsequent numbers from 6128-18 to 6128-26 are apparently vacant, and perhaps these were assigned to the photos in question. These conundrums remind us how much more we still have to learn about Tiffany's numbering systems.

When were the other photographs—those of the ceramics with bronze mountings and those of the glass—made? They seem to have been made all around the same time or slightly afterward, in late 1905 or 1906. As has been mentioned, the negative numbers that were assigned to these photographs are also part of the 6128 series. The suffixes for the glass continue the series directly, going from 6128-14 to 6128-17; the photos of the bronze-mounted pottery range from 6128-27 to 6128-30.

The photographs of the glass can be dated on the basis of one that includes a tall lava vase with spiral bands and irregularly placed "buttons" (page 185, top). This remarkably distinctive vase was included in Tiffany's display at the 1906 Paris Salon and is now in the Musée des Arts décoratifs, Paris

(see page 214). The vase had to be photographed in late 1905 or early 1906, prior to its leaving this country.[124] The other vases, with what are today referred to as "zipper" patterns, undoubtedly date from around the same time.

The pottery with bronze mounting is less easy to date, largely because we know so little about this type of ware. Only very few examples are known, suggesting that they were in limited production.[125] Of the vases photographed, the one with the motif of calla lilies is particularly notable because the blossoms were silvered for an additional coloristic effect (see page 213). It is possible that these experimental, elaborately handcrafted works preceded the more commercially oriented, electrodeposited wares, and thus would be dated prior to 1908. The fact that Nash penned "1915" on one of the photos is irrelevant, because he often erred, as was previously noted.

Even if all the photographs were made in the middle of the first decade of the twentieth century, this does not guarantee that the album was assembled at that time. One might still have lingering doubts and be tempted to veer toward a somewhat later date, after Leslie Nash's arrival at the factory. However, the absence of work from the later years of production argues against such an assumption. There are no examples of later glass, such as the aquamarine and paperweight varieties, and there is none of the all-over bronzed pottery that was introduced closer to 1908. For these reasons, we can conclude that the albums were assembled early on: first, the ceramics were photographed around 1905 or 1906, and the photos of the glass and bronzed pottery were incorporated shortly thereafter. In essence, we can reasonably assume that the albums were created before Leslie Nash took charge.

A   B   C   D   E

6128-2

A

B

6/28-3

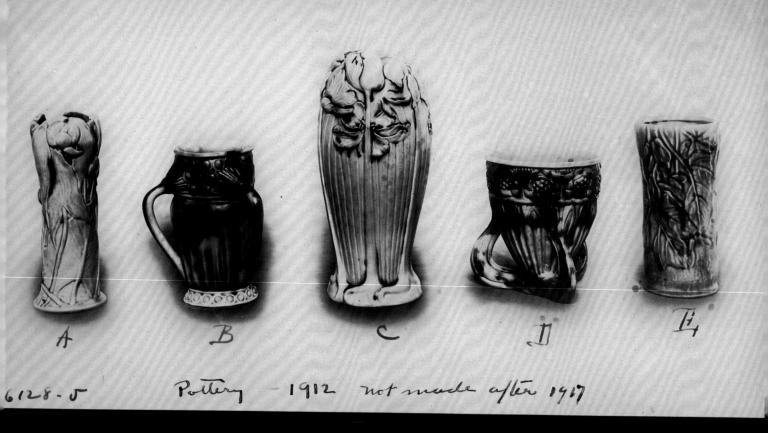

A   B   C   D   E

6128-5   Pottery – 1912   not made after 1917

A   B   C   D   E

6128-6

A   B   C   D   E

6128-11

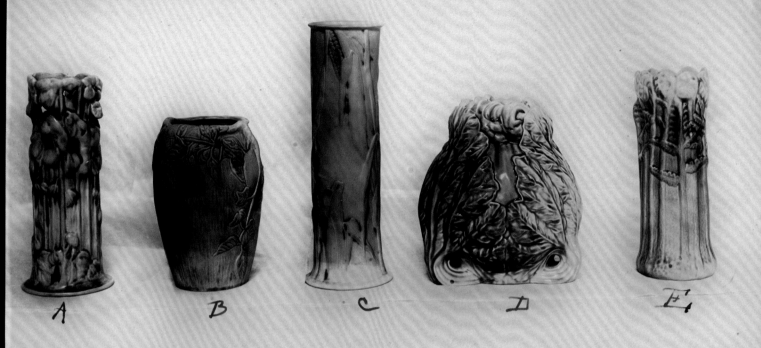

A   B   C   D   E

6128-13

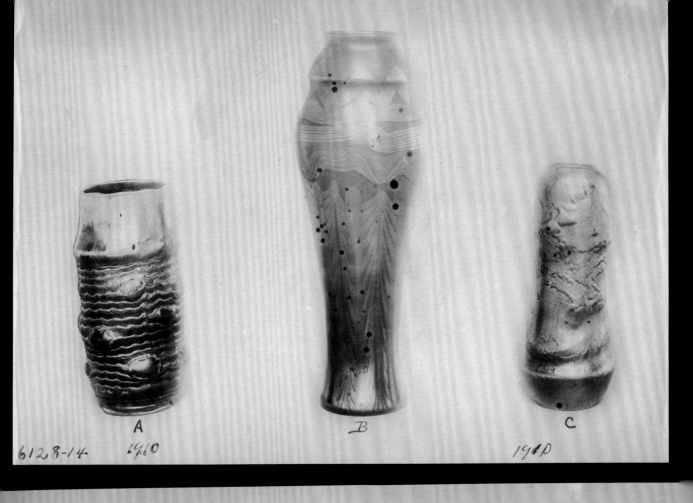

6128-14   1910

A   B   C   1910

6128-15   A   1920   B   C

6128-16

made 1916 and before

A.

B

6128-17

1912

Lamp shades - Hand carved &c &c &c

Designed by L H Nash.   1914 – 1917

6128-27

6128-28

BP

6128-29

Bronze
Pottery
1915

6128-30

PICTORIAL REVIEW

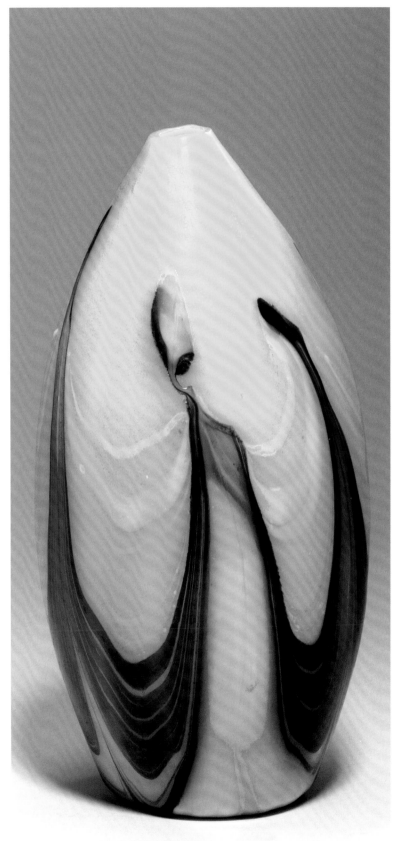

(RIGHT) GLASS VASE OF TEARDROP FORM, H. 7⅞ IN., c. 1892–93, WITH PAPER LABELS "TIFFANY FABRILE G . . ." AND "1293." NEW YORK, MACKLOWE GALLERY. PHOTO: CHRISTIE'S INC.

This vase appears in the photograph on page 71 of Nash's album of photographs of early glass (seen above). The "1293" registration numbers on the vase and on the shelf edge match exactly. The vase's "FABRILE" paper label records the earliest form of the Tiffany trade name, one which was probably used for less than a year. Vases of similar opaque yellow glass decorated with filaments of black and white are to be found in the Tokyo National Museum and other collections of early Tiffany glass.

These two vases of exceptional bravura figure on page 36 of Nash's album (seen at the left). Although that photograph is annotated "all AJN," implying that they entered Arthur J. Nash's collection, this does not seem correct. The vases went to two of Tiffany's major patrons: the one at the right went to Charles W. Gould, and the one at the left was bought by Henry O. Havemeyer. Likewise, Nash's annotation "1904" on his photograph is erroneous because this very photo was published in January 1896.

(BELOW LEFT) GLASS VASE WITH MARBLEIZED EFFECT, H. 4¹⁄₈ IN., c. 1893. NEW YORK, THE METROPOLITAN MUSEUM OF ART, GIFT OF H. O. HAVEMEYER, 1896 (96.17.31).
(BELOW RIGHT) GLASS VASE WITH MARBLEIZED EFFECT, H. 5¹⁄₄ IN., c. 1893. NEW YORK, THE METROPOLITAN MUSEUM OF ART, BEQUEST OF JAMES H. STUBBLEBINE, 1987 (1987.403.1). PHOTO: © 1989 THE METROPOLITAN MUSEUM OF ART

(LEFT) GLASS VASE OF DOUBLE GOURD FORM, H. 8 1/8 IN., c. 1893. NEW YORK, COLLECTION OF ERIC STREINER. PHOTO: CHRISTIE'S INC.

This vase with its interesting contrast of opaque and transparent glass can be seen above on page 73 of Nash's album of photographs. Another vase with this combination, pinched more like an hourglass, can be found in the collection that went to the Smithsonian Institution.

Large gourd forms are a particularly striking aspect of Tiffany's early glassware. The one at the right, of black opaque glass overlaid with threaded patterns, appears on page 38 of Nash's album, and a very similar example went to the Smithsonian Institution in 1896. The ribbed gourd at the far right is very similar but not identical to the vase pictured in the same early photograph. Hidden under the dark brown outer casing is an interior layer of bold chartreuse.

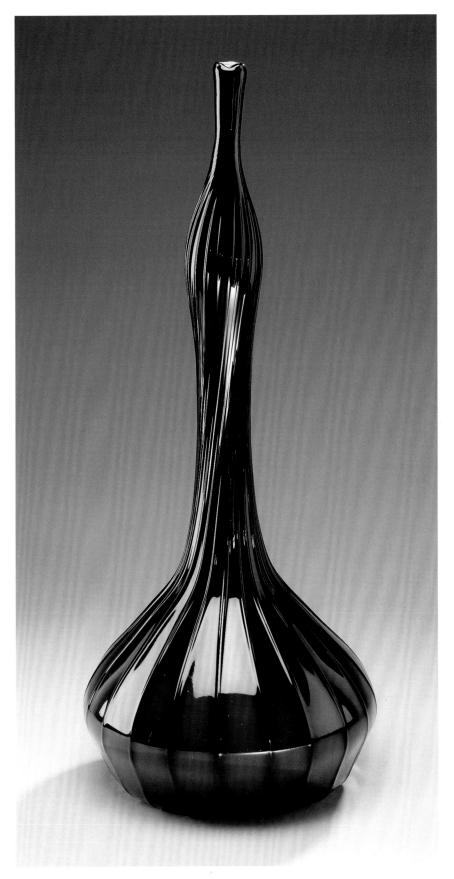

(RIGHT) FLOWER FORM GLASS VASE, MAT SURFACE, H. 12³/4 IN., c. 1893. PARIS, MUSÉE D'ORSAY. PHOTO: RÉUNION DES MUSÉES NATIONAUX/ART RESOURCE, NY. PHOTO BY JEAN SCHORMANS

(OPPOSITE PAGE, LEFT) FLOWER FORM GLASS VASE, MAT SURFACE, H. 117/16 IN., c. 1893. TOKYO, TOKYO NATIONAL MUSEUM.

(OPPOSITE PAGE, RIGHT) FLOWER FORM GLASS VASE WITH LOOPED STEM, MAT SURFACE, H. 107/8 IN., c. 1893. NEW YORK, COLLECTION OF ERIC STREINER. PHOTO: CHRISTIE'S INC.

Unlike the suave, elegant floriform vases that Tiffany's firm made later, many of his first essays in this genre were bold and erratic. Some, such as the one on this page, feature mat surfaces achieved by exposure to acid. Pictured on page 69 of Nash's album (seen at the top far right), it was among the first examples of glass that Tiffany sent to his European representative in Paris, S. Bing, who, in turn, sold it to the Musée du Luxembourg in 1894. The strangely attenuated version in Tokyo matches the one on page 89 of Nash's album (seen at the far right, middle row). Nash's annotation reveals that Tiffany kept one of this type for himself. The floriform with looped stem, originally owned by Sir William Van Horne—one of the founders of the Canadian Pacific Railway—does not exactly match any of those photographed, although the example on page 67 of Nash's album (seen at the bottom far right) is an extremely close "cousin."

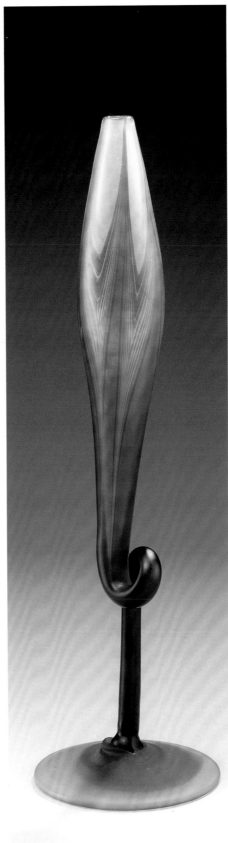

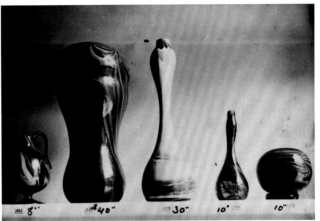

(OPPOSITE PAGE, LEFT) GLASS VASE OF DOUBLE GOURD FORM, H. 12¾ IN., c. 1893, WITH PAPER LABEL "1202." NEW YORK, COLLECTION OF ERIC STREINER. PHOTO: CHRISTIE'S INC.

(OPPOSITE PAGE, RIGHT) ROSEWATER SPRINKLER, GLASS WITH AVENTURINE, H. 13 IN., c. 1894–95, ENGRAVED "488." NEW YORK, COLLECTION OF ERIC STREINER. PHOTO: CHRISTIE'S INC.

(LEFT) RIBBED GLASS VASE OF DOUBLE GOURD FORM, H. 12³/₁₆ IN., c. 1893. BERLIN, STAATLICHE MUSEEN ZU BERLIN—PREUSSISCHER KULTURBESITZ, KUNSTGEWERBEMUSEUM.

Tiffany and Nash made a large number of these tall, gourd-shaped bottle forms from richly marbleized glass. The one at the left, bought in New York in 1893 by the Berlin Kunstgewerbemuseum, closely resembles the one depicted on page 39 of Nash's album, as seen above. Although a large number of rosewater sprinklers appear in Nash's photographs, none corresponds to the one in the Streiner collection. Its distinctive, richly grained glass of reddish bronze is heightened by the inclusion of aventurine.

(OPPOSITE) GLASS BOWL WITH PULLED FEATHER DECORATION, H. 5 1/16 IN., c. 1894–95, ENGRAVED "145." BERLIN, STAATLICHE MUSEEN ZU BERLIN—PREUSSISCHER KULTURBESITZ, KUNSTGEWERBEMUSEUM.

(LEFT) GLASS VASE WITH FEATHERED DECORATION, H. 8 IN., c. 1893. NEW YORK, COLLECTION OF ERIC STREINER. PHOTO: CHRISTIE'S INC.

These two vessels, made from the same striated ochre glass with feathered green decoration, correspond to works photographed in Nash's album—the bowl on page 56 and the vase on page 67. A series of closed forms resembling globular fruit were also made from the same combination of glass batches; many can be seen in Nash's photos, and a few have survived, including one in the Tokyo Imperial Museum.

A great revelation in the Nash archives is the wealth of beautiful preliminary drawings made in the enameling department. While some charming watercolor renderings of plants have survived, until now we did not know of any designs for specific objects. This watercolor is of particular interest because of its many annotations. At the very top is the work number "SG 44." This is the numbering system used by the Stourbridge Glass Company enameling department, and it is engraved on the actual bowl as well. These marks assure us that both the watercolor and the bowl had to have been executed prior to 1902, when the Stourbridge Glass Company was renamed Tiffany Furnaces. At the lower left of the watercolor is the signature of one of the chief figures in the enameling department, Julia Munson, and above her signature are her indications of which color enamels she intended to use. At the upper right is her record of the fifty hours between

April 10 and 19 that she spent laboring to complete the project; the cost of Tiffany's objects was generally determined by the cost of the materials and by the number of hours expended. The right side of the drawing shows an alteration in the profile of the shape and an indication that the drawing was to be taken to "George," who was to create the copper blank. The one specious element is Leslie Nash's signature at the bottom. This was added many decades later when he decided to sign all of "his" designs, so as to take back some of the credit that had been given to Tiffany and not to the Nashes.

Pottery.

LESLIE HNASH

(OPPOSITE PAGE) MAQUETTE FOR AN ENAMELED VASE WITH SKUNK CABBAGE MOTIF, WATERCOLOR OVER PENCIL, 10 5/8 X 8 IN., c. 1898–1900. ESTATE OF LESLIE H. NASH. PHOTO: CHRISTIE'S INC.

(ABOVE LEFT) ENAMELED VASE WITH SKUNK CABBAGE MOTIF, H. 7½ IN., ENGRAVED "LOUIS C. TIFFANY" AND "SG58." WHEREABOUTS UNKNOWN. PHOTO: CHRISTIE'S IMAGES, NEW YORK 1980

(ABOVE RIGHT) POTTERY VASE WITH SKUNK CABBAGE MOTIF, H. 6⅛ IN., c. 1904–10, ENGRAVED "P1220 L. C. TIFFANY—FAVRILE POTTERY" AND INCISED WITH "LCT" MONOGRAM. NEW YORK, COLLECTION OF ERIC STREINER. PHOTO: CHRISTIE'S INC.

Although this beautiful rendering was signed in pencil by Nash, the watercolor was probably made a decade before he began working for Tiffany. It represents an early stage of design where the closure at the top seems to have been left unresolved. The actual enamel (bearing the early registration number "SG58") shows how the leaves were ultimately brought together to form a more continuous lip, and the colors were heightened from the strangely melancholic blues and purples of the watercolor. A ceramic version was then made using this later design. Nash penciled in the word "Pottery" at the lower right, perhaps wrongly thinking that this was a design for the ceramic version; he would have known that version for no other reason than that he had photographs of it. But he later corrected himself and penned in, "Also made in copper enameled," unintentionally inverting the sequence; the enameled version always preceded the ceramic version.

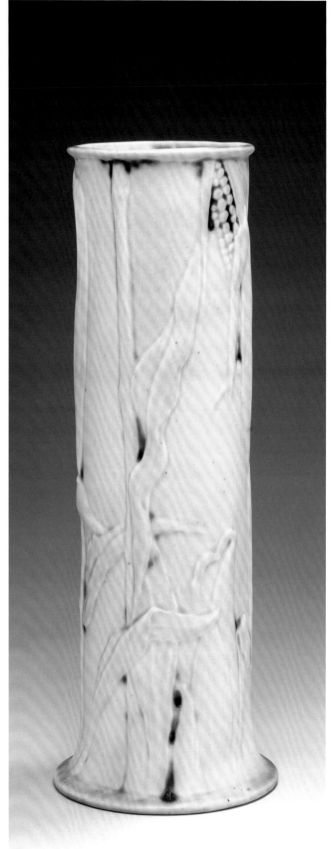

(RIGHT) POTTERY VASE WITH CORNSTALK MOTIF, H. 12⅝ IN., c. 1904, INCISED WITH "LCT" MONOGRAM. NEW YORK, PRIVATE COLLECTION. PHOTO: CHRISTIE'S INC.

A comparison of this ceramic with its counterpart in Nash's album reveals that this is the vase that was photographed. The glaze in both falls in exactly the same way, highlighting the identical kernels of corn and leaves. In this instance, we happen to know the vase's provenance—namely, that it came from the estate of Joseph Briggs, the manager of the mosaic department and last business manager of Tiffany Studios. He reputedly received six thousand dollars' worth of stock when Louis C. Tiffany Furnaces, Inc., went into bankruptcy.

Tiffany particularly favored humble plants from the garden and the forest. The crinkled, leafy motif on this vase suggests something of a Savoy cabbage, and in this respect, it is useful to recall Leslie Nash's description of how, every Monday, Tiffany brought any flower, vine, bean, and cabbage that interested him, and he then had his artists work these subjects into decorative schemes.

The glaze on this vase was likened at the time to "old ivory," because in those areas where it was applied thinly it has a slightly yellow cast, whereas it wells up in the crevices to appear almost black, much like the color of aged ivory. Because the glaze was intentionally applied unevenly, the effect could be quite different from vase to vase, as can be seen by comparing the example here with the one photographed in the Nash album.

(BELOW) POTTERY VASE WITH CABBAGE MOTIF, H. 8½ IN., c. 1904–10, INSCRIBED "P273 TIFFANY–FAVRILE–POTTERY" AND INCISED WITH "LCT" MONOGRAM. NEW YORK, PRIVATE COLLECTION. PHOTO: CHRISTIE'S INC.

An extremely similar but not identical covered bowl appears in a photograph in Nash's album. The enameled version of this bowl (numbered SG43) is in the Chrysler Museum of Art in Norfolk, Virginia. In adapting the design to the ceramic medium, certain changes had to be effected: notably the openwork on the lid was reduced so that it could be fired successfully.

(BELOW) COVERED POTTERY BOWL WITH VIRGINIA CREEPER MOTIF, H. 6½ IN., C. 1904–10, INCISED WITH "LCT" MONOGRAM. NEW YORK, PRIVATE COLLECTION. PHOTO: CHRISTIE'S INC.

(LEFT) POTTERY VASE WITH JACK-IN-THE-PULPIT MOTIF, H. 11 3/8 IN., c. 1904–10, INCISED WITH "LCT" MONOGRAM. NEW YORK, PRIVATE COLLECTION. PHOTO: CHRISTIE'S INC.

This vase once belonged to A. Douglas Nash and then was in the collection of Albert Christian Revi. Revi reported that live plants were shellacked and then electroplated to create the models for such ceramics, which is an interesting tale but not necessarily true. This particular design, as with most early ceramics, was executed first as an enameled copper vase (numbered SG 101), which is now in the Louis C. Tiffany Garden Museum, Matsue, Japan.

(RIGHT) POTTERY VASE WITH PARROT TULIP MOTIF, H. 11½ IN., c. 1904–10, INCISED WITH "LCT" MONOGRAM. NEW YORK, PRIVATE COLLECTION. PHOTO: CHRISTIE'S INC.

The second type of glaze that was developed for Tiffany's ceramics is this type of mossy green. Its soft, semigloss green is flecked irregularly with a darker green, creating a gentle, organic effect like moss growing on a rock. Whereas Tiffany generally preferred a relatively straightforward approach to nature, the repetitive rhythmical flourishes at the bottom of the vase hint at the Art Nouveau style.

212

(LEFT) POTTERY VASE WITH PARTIALLY SILVERED BRONZE MOUNTING, CALLA LILY MOTIF, H. 15 1/2 IN., C. 1905, INCISED WITH "LCT" MONOGRAM AND "7" IN THE CERAMIC, ENGRAVED "LOUIS C. TIFFANY" AND STAMPED "FAVRILE 104" IN THE MOUNTING. PRIVATE COLLECTION. PHOTO: CHRISTIE'S INC.

This and two other ceramic vases with elaborate cages of decorative bronze mounts were photographed by Tiffany. Another extant example of a ceramic mounted with a bronze, cagelike, floral design is in the collection of the Charles Hosmer Morse Museum, Winter Park, Florida, and it is marked "FAVRILE 102," thereby suggesting the limited extent of this line of experimentation.

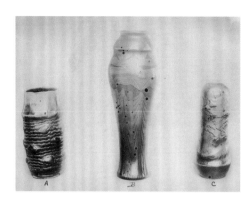

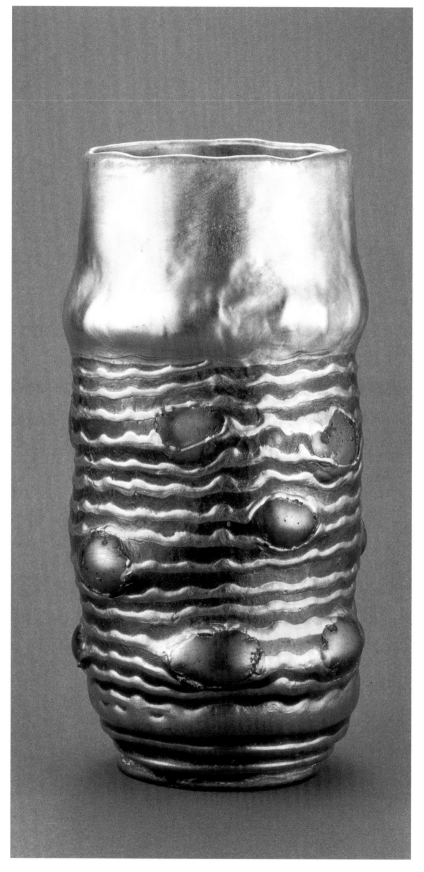

(RIGHT) GLASS VASE, H. 9¹/₁₆ IN., c. 1906, ENGRAVED "L. C. TIFFANY FAVRILE, SALON 1906" AND "2023C." PARIS, MUSÉE DES ARTS DÉCORATIFS. PHOTO: LAURENT-SULLY JAULMES, ALL RIGHTS RESERVED

Vases with such thick appliqués of lustrous gold glass were dubbed "lava" and represent one of the boldest innovations of Tiffany Furnaces. This particularly striking lava vase can be seen in several of the photographs of the exhibition vitrine at the Paris 1906 Salon, including one among Nash's papers (which he wrongly identified as the Buffalo Pan-American Exhibition of 1901). The vase stayed in Paris and was officially donated by Tiffany to the Musée des Arts décoratifs the following year, 1907. Thus, the firm's photograph of it must have been made in the United States and prior to 1907.

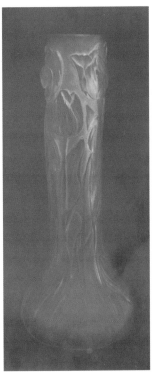

(LEFT) GLASS ROCK CRYSTAL CAMEO VASE, H. 16½ IN., c. 1909, ENGRAVED "L. C. TIFFANY FAVRILE 223D," WITH GOLD PAPER LABEL "1904." NORFOLK, VIRGINIA, CHRYSLER MUSEUM OF ART, GIFT OF WALTER P. CHRYSLER, JR., 71.6300.

Leslie Nash described the development of carved Rock Crystal vases as Arthur J. Nash's "last creative effort." The thick glass was designed to have an opalescent luminosity and was then laboriously carved by a trained technician. Leslie noted that one of these vases took over 180 hours to carve, which accounted for its high price. Nash's photograph, shown above, of an almost identical vase is marked on the reverse side, "Tulip—16 $37500 design AJ Nash First prize Alaskan Youkon Ex Rock Crystal." The front side of the photo records the registration number "224D." Clearly, the two vases were made in close sequence to each other and the other examples that Nash intended to illustrate in his book (see page 67).

(LEFT) SAMIAN RED TEL-EL-AMARNA GLASS VASE, H. 10¹³⁄₁₆ IN., c. 1908, ENGRAVED "L. C. TIFFANY" AND "5018E." HAWORTH ART GALLERY, ACCRINGTON, LANCASHIRE (HYNDBURN BOROUGH COUNCIL).

(RIGHT) SAMIAN RED GLASS VASE, H. 8⁷⁄₈ IN., c. 1915, ENGRAVED "1575J L. C. TIFFANY—FAVRILE." NORFOLK, VIRGINIA, CHRYSLER MUSEUM OF ART, GIFT OF WALTER P. CHRYSLER, JR. 71.6244.

One of the new colors introduced after 1900 was the so-called Samian Red, though how it is to be distinguished from Tiffany's other reds is not certain. Many of the Samian Red vases, such as the one at the right, were graceful, unornamented Oriental shapes; Leslie Nash had a vase of this form (see page 225). The Samian Red generally was not combined with other colors, except for discreetly feathered Tel-el-Amarna patterns such as the one around the neck of the vase now in the Haworth Art Gallery, and formerly in Joseph Briggs' collection.

In the years after 1900, one of the preoccupations of Tiffany Furnaces was the creation of floral ornament through the use of millefiore and other techniques, and encasing this within heavy glass, as in the paperweight tradition. The idea for such vases may have been sparked at the turn of the century, as seen in an example with morning glories and a stunning gold interior in the collection of the Musée d'Orsay. The floral motif had such staying power that variants were executed for exhibitions over the next decade and a half. An impressive display of these vases was shown at the Paris Salon of 1914, and then again at the Panama-Pacific Exhibition in San Francisco in 1915.

(RIGHT) GLASS VASE OF PAPERWEIGHT TECHNIQUE WITH MORNING GLORY MOTIF, H. 10 IN., c. 1913–14, ENGRAVED "L. C. TIFFANY—FAVRILE 8559H PARIS-SALON 1914." CORNING, NEW YORK, CORNING MUSEUM OF GLASS, GIFT OF MR. AND MRS. HOWARD STEIN. PHOTO: CHRISTIE'S IMAGES, NEW YORK 1995

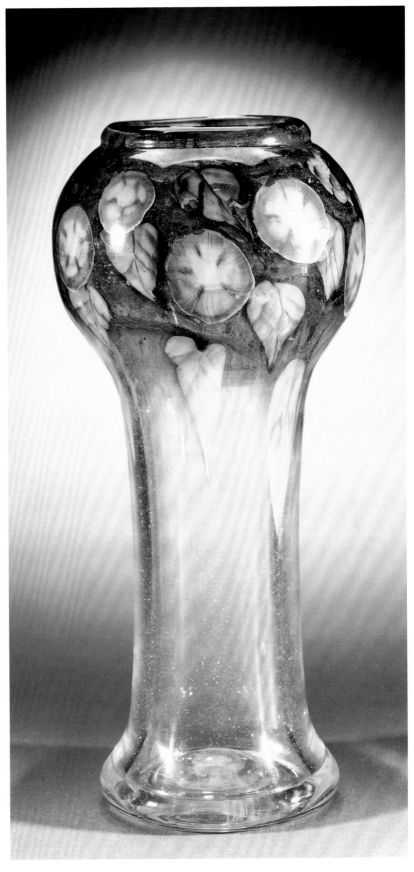

MAQUETTES FOR ENAMELED PIN CUSHIONS, BOX COVERS, ETC., WATERCOLOR OVER
PENCIL, IN LESLIE H. NASH'S SCRAPBOOK, "TIFFANY FAVRILE GLASS & METAL
PRODUCTS . . . ," c. 1908–12. PARSIPPANY, NEW JERSEY, COLLECTION OF TIFFANY & CO.
ARCHIVES. PHOTO: CHRISTIE'S IMAGES, NEW YORK 2000

Leslie Nash's annotations on the two pages seen above are
almost as interesting as the beautiful watercolor renderings
that are pasted down here. At the left, he claims that these
were among his first designs for enamels and that he himself executed the first "samples." His observation at the right
side, about reducing costs through the use of acid rather
than hand cutting to perforate the copper, suggests the
practical, economical side of his approach to business.

Despite Leslie Nash's signature on the watercolor design, seen above, the covered jar was made almost a decade before his arrival at Tiffany. An early dating is assured by two marks on the underside of the jar: first, a registration number in the 20,000 range, referring to a numerical system abandoned around the turn of the century, and second, the Stourbridge Glass Company registration number, which was not employed after 1902. The drawing is annotated "Too dark," and in fact, the finished vase is brighter; the leaves are a more lively green, and the squash flower a richer orange-yellow. Louis C. Tiffany seems to have liked the result, and he kept the jar for himself at Laurelton Hall. The drawings on the right page record Leslie Nash's invention of prongs for the backs of glass tiles, which bond the tile to the plaster or mortar of the wall. Typical of his less optimistic mood in his later years, there are the sadly ironic comments on the left page: "Even I make mistakes—think of that—I hate water color—runs all over the place."

Leslie Nash wrote at great length about this commemorative piece (see page 90). As we know from a printed notice of the time, it was commissioned by Earle E. Carley and was made by Tiffany Furnaces from shards of the glasses used to toast the recipient at a bachelor's dinner given in his honor on June 20, 1919. Strangely, Nash misremembered the recipient's name as "Lucius Boomer." The error is even more curious because Leslie's father, Arthur J. Nash, was a good friend of Bowman and together with the architect John Petit often lunched with him at Keen's Chop House and at the Waldorf. Moreover, Leslie was frequently invited to join the party.

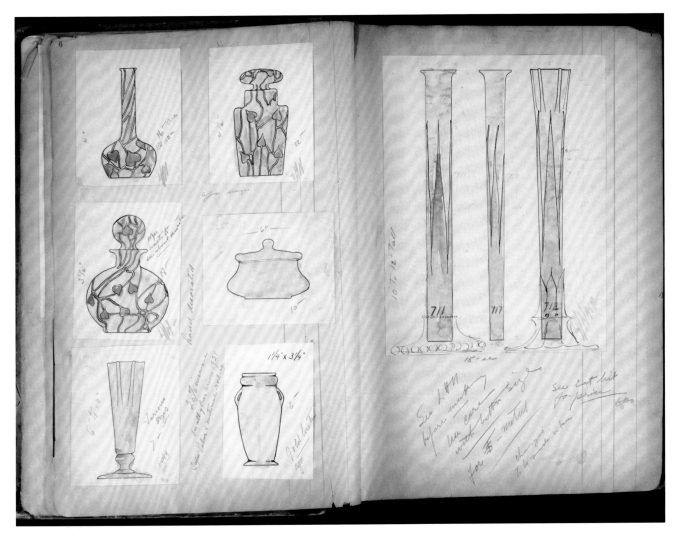

DRAWINGS FOR GLASS TO BE PRODUCED SERIALLY, WATERCOLOR OVER PENCIL, IN LESLIE H. NASH'S SCRAPBOOK, "TIFFANY FAVRILE GLASS & METAL PRODUCTS . . . ," c. 1912–20. PARSIPPANY, NEW JERSEY, COLLECTION OF TIFFANY & CO. ARCHIVES. PHOTO: CHRISTIE'S IMAGES, NEW YORK 2000

Although *iridescence* and *Tiffany glass* are almost synonymous in the public's eye, in the beginning and in accord with both Tiffany's and Arthur J. Nash's wishes, this effect was used with great restraint as a limited part of the ornament. Later, in response to public demand, vessels with all-over gold or blue luster were used, sometimes with a simple pattern of green trailing vines and leaves. The cylindrical forms at the right were designed to be inserted in bronze feet made by Tiffany Studios. The ever-practical Nash was quite happy with the financial profit that all such commercial glassware brought.

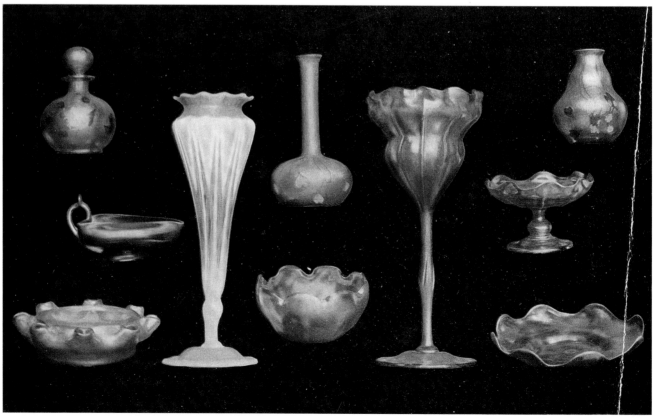

(ABOVE AND OPPOSITE PAGE) FAVRILE GLASSWARE FOR THE GERMAN MARKET, c. 1916.
ESTATE OF LESLIE H. NASH. PHOTO: CHRISTIE'S INC.

Another of the revelations from Leslie Nash's manuscript and scrapbook is that Tiffany Furnaces conducted an export business, selling to Germany. The objects had to be relatively small and unornamented (or decorated simply) to overcome the costs of transport and import duties, and thus remain affordable in the marketplace. These printed catalogue sheets and price list are our sole witnesses to another aspect of Tiffany's empire.

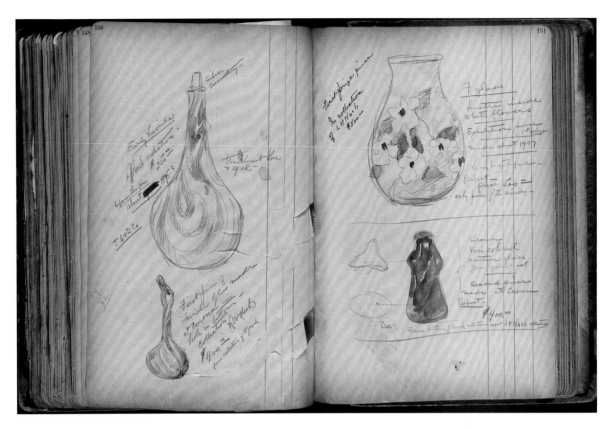

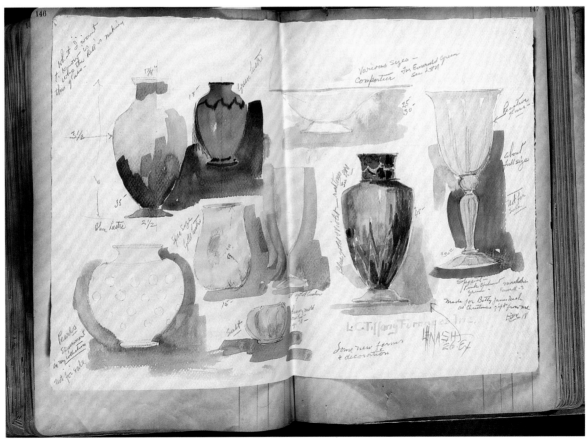

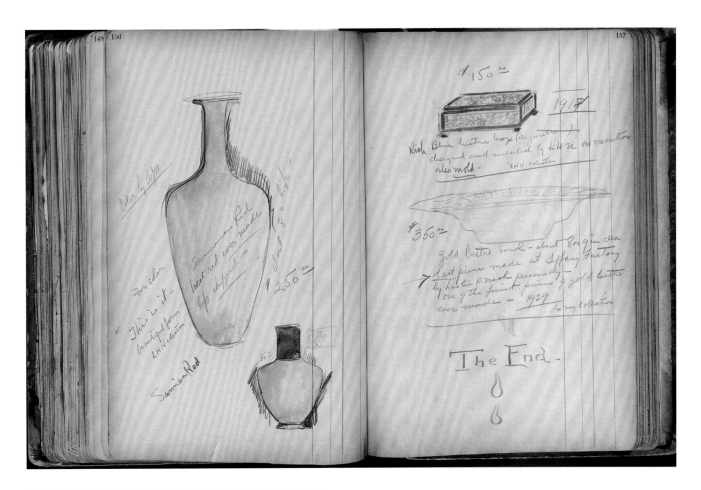

The Nashes, father and son, retained examples of the company's glassmaking and, in effect, created a virtual history of the development of Tiffany glass. Unfortunately, most of it was sold in 1965, after Leslie's death, to Mr. and Mrs. Neil Reisner. Recorded here are examples of various innovations and stages in the development of Favrile glass. The first two pages include three examples of the earliest glass, including what Leslie claimed to be the first two pieces blown at the Corona plant. The penultimate page shows two examples of Samian Red glass, one of which Leslie claimed was the finest ever made. The last page shows a bronze box, supposedly made in 1918, whose sides and cover are made with iridescent blue glass panels designed by Nash, and a gold iridescent bowl, supposedly from 1925, which was the "<u>last</u> piece made at Tiffany Factory." The tears descending from the words *The End* can be interpreted in various ways—as the sadness felt at the end of this era of beautiful glass or perhaps as an expression of Leslie Nash's general bitterness.

NOTES

1. New York, Christie's, December 8, 2000, lots 301–11.

2. Written in the left margin in Leslie's hand: "My thoughts are here but." Written at the top but not by Leslie: "Prior to '6th Writing.' "

3. The following three lines are crossed out and not fully legible: "Father and four uncles—[illegible] Matthew, Mark, Luke, John and Jessie—all ministers of [illegible]."

4. Nash's citation of the last three names is incorrect. The actual sequence was Tiffany Furnaces (1902) and Louis C. Tiffany Furnaces, Inc. (1920). As far as is known, there was no company with the name "L. C. Tiffany Furnaces, Inc."

5. This complaint makes little sense, at least at first glance, since the Nash name was not in any of the companies' names. Leslie's intent was clearer in an earlier draft of his manuscript: "It is easy to see that as we progressed, Mr. Tiffany wanted to be the only person *who should receive credit for glass, invented by Arthur J. Nash.*"

6. These two sentences are essential for understanding why Leslie Nash's signature appears on so many watercolor renderings that he himself did not execute and that were, in fact, made even a decade before he joined the firm.

7. See pp. 36 and note 60, where his relation to the two Webb glasshouses is discussed in greater detail.

8. See a typed manuscript, "Arthur John Nash," to be found among the early drafts for his book, still with the Nash family.

9. Leslie Nash's account in the Early Glass Album, 99, reports that the family lived first in "Brooklyn—for about one year—then to Flushing, a short time in Corona, L.I. while Factory was being built then back to Flushing L.I. N.Y."

10. Other members of the Nash family believed that Arthur Nash was a partner, perhaps an equal partner, and that the factory had been Nash's property before Tiffany came on the scene; see Albert Christian Revi, *American Art Nouveau Glass* (Exton, PA: 1968), 25.

11. A. Stuart Patterson owned 38 shares; George Holmes and Arthur J. Nash each owned one share. After a June 1893 stock increase, Charles Lewis Tiffany and Charles T. Cook (president of Tiffany & Co.) were also listed as stockholders, probably due to their supplying the needed capital. See Revi, *American Art Nouveau Glass,* 22.

12. See Revi, *American Art Nouveau Glass,* 22.

13. Despite modern characterizations of Nash as a "wizard with a blowpipe," he did not have such skills; see Robert Koch, *Tiffany's Glass—Bronzes—Lamps* (New York: 1971), 65.

14. See pp. 37–39.

15. For example, glassblower Jimmy Stewart recalled that when the first iridescent glass was produced in 1895, Tiffany was in his office together with his chemist (McIlhinney) and Arthur J. Nash, suggesting that there was more of a collaborative effort than is indicated by Leslie Nash. See Koch, *Tiffany's Glass—Bronzes—Lamps,* 64.

16. See Janet Zapata, *The Jewelry and Enamels of Louis Comfort Tiffany* (New York: 1993), 139 and passim.

17. Written in a letter from Frederick Carder to Leslie C. Byer, dated August 30, 1944, and sent to Nash on September 12, 1944. Tiffany initiated a suit against Carder's employer—the Steuben Glass Works in Corning, New York—in November 1913. The suit was settled out of court, and stopped in March 1914. Zapata, *The Jewelry and Enamels of Louis Comfort Tiffany,* 139, notes that McIlhinney remained on the payroll of Tiffany & Co. until August 1914.

18. Elsewhere, Leslie claims that his mother, Fannie St. Clare Taylor Nash, was left without means, and thus he wrote Tiffany seeking financial help but he received no reply.

19. The last section of the paragraph, beginning here, has the marginal note "re-write/mixed up."

20. For photographs of the fountain, see Henry H. Saylor, "The Country Home of Mr. Louis C. Tiffany," *Country Life in America* 15 (December 1908), 162, and Robert Koch, *Louis C. Tiffany, Rebel in Glass,* (New York: 1964), 204.

21. Tiffany kept a nominal share for himself and gave his foundation the remaining 110 shares. Arthur J. Nash still owned 15 shares; A. Douglas Nash, who served as secretary, owned 22, and Leslie owned 18. There were also some minor shareholders. Tiffany's son, Charles L., owned 5 shares; George F. Heydt of Tiffany & Co. owned 1 share, and Joseph Briggs, manager of the mosaic department at Tiffany Studios, owned 8 shares. Thus, in actuality, the Nashes did not own the dominant portion.

22. One of his captions (p. 43), for example, says that the factory closed in 1929. This is also indicated on the title design (p. 25).

23. Recorded on page 47 of an early manuscript version of his book, still with the Nash estate.

24. The last listing for A. Douglas Nash in the Queens telephone directory is in the winter 1930–31 edition (corrected to November 25, 1930). Tiffany Studios filed for bankruptcy on April 16, 1932.

25. The first listing for the firm appears in the summer 1929 Queens telephone directory (corrected to June 15, 1929). However, it was not listed in the winter 1929–30 issue (corrected to December 14, 1929).

26. Scrapbook (*Tiffany Favrile Glass & Metal Products*), 142.

27. Although Tiffany was reputedly proud to have Theodore Roosevelt as his neighbor in Oyster Bay, it was this same president who about 1904 ordered the demolition of Tiffany's early decorations for the White House.

28. See above, p. 5.

29. Scrapbook, on the unnumbered first page of the book.

30. Scrapbook, 106.

31. Scrapbook, 129. In a postscript, Nash added, "I guess he means well."

32. Scrapbook, 102.

33. René de Quélin, "A Many-Sided Creator of the Beautiful: The Work of Louis Comfort Tiffany by an Associate," *Arts and Decoration* 17 (July 1922), 176.

34. *Exhibition of L'Art Nouveau, S. Bing, Paris,* exh. cat. (London: Grafton Galleries, 1899), 14–18.

35. W. R. Bradshaw, "Favrile Glass," *House Beautiful* 7 (April 1900), 276.

36. Charles de Kay's nephew, Rodman de Kay Gilder, married Tiffany's daughter, Louise Comfort, on December 10, 1910.

37. Charles de Kay, *The Art Work of Louis C. Tiffany* (New York: 1914), 19.

38. This description was recorded by Albert Christian Revi, *Nineteenth Century Glass, Its Genesis and Development* (New York, Edinburgh, and Toronto: 1959), 114, after he had interviewed Nash.

39. Thelma Shull, "L. C. Tiffany and Favrile Glass," *Hobbies* (July 1942), 47, 58–59; Dorothea M. Fox, "Tiffany Glass," *Antiques* 44 (November and December), 240–41, 295–96.

40. See, for example, Edgar Kaufmann, Jr., "Tiffany, Then and Now," *Interiors* 114 (February 1955), 82–85. Kaufmann was also a collector of Tiffany glass and objects, along with Joseph H. Heil and other influential New York cognoscenti. See also Helen and George S. McKearin, *Two Hundred Years of American Blown Glass* (New York: 1950), 135–36.

41. Gertrude Speenburgh, *The Arts of the Tiffanys* (Chicago: 1956).

42. Larry Freeman, *Iridescent Glass* (Watkins Glen, N.Y.: 1956), 19.

43. See the letter from Leslie Byer to Leslie Nash dated November 27, 1956. Although the title page of the final typescript bears the date 1957, the editing went on after this date. Leslie Nash continued to correct some of the pages, which were then removed and replaced (according to John Nash's annotation on the removed pages) with the newly typed versions in March 1958—that is, the month after Leslie's death.

44. See Herbert Weissberger, "After Many Years: Tiffany Glass," *Carnegie Magazine* 30 (October 1956), 265–68, 279.

45. Revi, *Nineteenth Century Glass,* 226–27.

46. Koch's letters to Leslie Nash, dated December 28, 1956, and February 2, 1957. Although Koch wrote that he had more questions to pose in the future, there was no further correspondence. Koch's published view was that though "the Nashes admittedly received little or no credit in the promotion efforts of Tiffany's firm," and that some of the credit for the superior quality of the glass was due to Arthur Nash, nonetheless, "it is to Tiffany that one must attribute the unique quality of the designs"; see Koch, *Rebel in Glass,* 126–27. Because Koch's book did not appear until 1964, well after Leslie's death, Leslie was spared reading this generally balanced opinion.

47. Koch (letter of February 2, 1957) wrote that he was also "green" about publishing, that one shouldn't expect much money, and that he had the advantage of being young and working for an accredited college. Leslie Nash was seventy years old, and he had no connections with publishers or institutions.

48. Letter of H. B. Brownell of Doubleday & Company to Leslie Nash, June 21, 1957.

49. Robert Koch, *Stained Glass Decades,* Ph.D. thesis, Yale University, New Haven, CT, 1957.

50. A small exhibition catalogue was published. Arthur J. Nash was mentioned only as having directed the glassblowing division, and Tiffany was once again credited with the lion's share of the success of the firm.

51. Interview between Jimmy Stewart and Robert Koch, April 6, 1966, transcribed in Koch, *Louis C. Tiffany's Glass—Bronzes—Lamps,* 65.

52. See p. 46.

53. For example, see the interview with glassblower Jimmy Stewart in Koch, *Louis C. Tiffany's Glass—Bronzes—Lamps,* 62–83; see also the collection of photographs owned by Maurice Kelly, sold New York, Christie's, June 13, 1987, lot 185.

54. See Revi, *American Art Nouveau Glass,* 25–26. That the two tellings of the tale concur assures us of the relative accuracy of some of the stories remembered by the Nash family.

55. For the denial by A. Douglas Nash's widow, see Revi, *American Art Nouveau Glass,* 27.

56. Cecilia Waern, "The Industrial Arts of America: II. The Tiffany or 'Favrile' Glass," *Studio* 14 (July 1898), 16.

57. Nash made just the opposite charge elsewhere in his manuscript (see p. 96), complaining that Tiffany always came back from Europe brimming over with ideas to experiment. He had so many ideas and so much work, in fact, that this ultimately caused Nash to have a nervous breakdown.

58. Typed across the bottom of the page is the declaration: "THIS MANUSCRIPT IS NOW THE PROPERTY OF BETTY J. NASH, SAYVILLE, LI." referring to Leslie Nash's widow. In the top left and right corners is the stamped, subsequent declaration of his son: "JOHN W. NASH/ 72 SAXTON AVE./ SAYVILLE, N.Y."

59. The page numbers here correspond to the present publication. Because the order of some of the photographs has been shifted slightly to accommodate the design of this publication, the table of contents has been modified accordingly. References to deleted photographs have been omitted. Topics included in the manuscript but not listed here by Nash have been inserted within brackets.

60. Elsewhere, as we have already witnessed (see pp. 4–5), Leslie Nash emphasized his father's position by describing him as a partner in Webb's firm. According to Jason Ellis, "Glassmakers of Stourbridge and Dudley 1612–1992" (manuscript, Broadfield House Glass Museum, Kingswinford, England), documentary evidence shows that Nash was the manager for Edward Webb (c. 1875–c.1887) and that among his patented designs were ones for Vasa Murrinha glassware (1882), Worcester Ivory Glass (1883), and Dresden Cameo (1885). About 1887, Nash joined Thomas Webb & Sons at the Dennis Glassworks. Another account was given by Frederick Carder in a letter to Leslie C. Byer dated June 19, 1942, a copy of which is in the Nash estate: "[M]y acquaintance with Arthur Nash was rather limited. . . . [H]e was at one time connected with Edward Webb & Sons of the White House Glass Works of Wordsley, England. He came to them from Birmingham where he had been a copper plate engraver. Webb & Sons got him to execute copper plates for transfer printing onto glass and then to etch same with fluoric acid, such as monograms, badges and other ornamental designs. After some years with them he became manager and experimented with various colored glasses."

61. Carder's letter to Byer of June 19, 1942, gives a different and perhaps more accurate assessment of why Nash left Webb: "Owing to some misunderstanding with Messrs. Webb he left England and came to America."

62. There are other reports of Tiffany buying a factory in Boston for the window department and the development of bronze-clad leading.

63. Although the Nash family frequently claimed that Nash was a partner in the company, this idea does not appear in most scholarship on the Tiffany Glass and Decorating Company. It is significant that when the Corona factory was consumed by fire, Nash is reputed to have said to his wife, "Fannie, there goes my last dollar." See p. 42.

64. The Tiffany Glass and Decorating Company was officially incorporated on February 18, 1892.

65. When the Stourbridge Glass Company was incorporated on April 7, 1893, Arthur Nash and Georges Holmes each owned only one share, whereas A. Stuart Patterson, who served as secretary of the firm, owned thirty-eight. Louis C. Tiffany's name does not appear as an affiliated party. An increase in capitalization that was voted in June 1893 lists Tiffany's father, Charles L. Tiffany, and Charles T. Cook, president of Tiffany & Co., as stockholders. Another certificate of stock increase in September 1893 designated Louis C. Tiffany as president, the first time his name appeared in association with this undertaking. For this corporate history, see Revi, *American Art Nouveau Glass,* 22.

66. Nash has elided two changes of the corporate name. On September 29, 1902, the Stourbridge Glass Company was renamed Tiffany Furnaces. Many years later—on January 6, 1920—that name was changed to Louis C. Tiffany Furnaces, Inc. Also see above, p. 5 and note 4.

67. Arthur Nash's formula book, frequently cited by Leslie, cannot be traced at present but is believed to be extant, perhaps owned by one of Arthur Nash's grandsons or other descendants. As early as the 1930s, it was claimed that Tiffany had destroyed his secret formulas. See "Famous Favrile Glass Production Held Lost," *New York Tribune,* June 2, 1936; also *American Collector* 5 (April 1936), 2. When Revi interviewed the Nash family, he learned of Nash's coded formula books, and Leslie must have told how he had perused them (though the widow of Arthur Douglas Nash claimed she had never seen any such books); see Revi, *American Art Nouveau Glass,* 27. At least two of the workmen, George Joseph Cook and Arthur Saunders, had their own notebooks with Tiffany glass formulas; see Koch, *Louis C. Tiffany's Glass—Bronzes—Lamps,* 74–75.

68. Arthur Nash's early involvement with dresses of glass fiber while in England may be relevant to his later seeking employment with the Libbey Glass Company. The American company exhibited lampshades with spun-glass fabric at the World Columbian Exposition of 1893 in Chicago, and subsequently made dresses of the material; see Revi, *Nineteenth Century Glass,* 120–22. "Glass Dress Paris 88 Ex Spun Glass" was the topic of a story that Nash intended to write, as recorded in his memorandum at the back of the album with photographs of early glass.

69. The exact date of the fire was October 28, 1893; see "Disastrous Fire at Corona," *Newtown Register,* November 2, 1893; "A Life Lost in a Fire," *Long Island Farmer,* November 3, 1893. In an earlier draft, Leslie wrote, "As I recall the factory started making glass in the latter part of 1892 or early 1893. One year it was burned to the ground, leaving the large melting furnace still standing." Jimmy Stewart, a Tiffany glassblower, had thought the factory fire occurred in 1893; see Koch, *Tiffany's Glass—Bronzes—Lamps,* 63. However, Stewart began working for Tiffany only in 1895, and thus he was not a firsthand witness. His description of the building as having been a former laundry is open to question; traditionally, it has been claimed that Tiffany had first rented a laundry in Brooklyn and then moved to the Corona site.

70. In an early draft, Leslie wrote, "[T]he entire building was rebuilt. . . . It was financed by Mr. Chas. L. Tiffany, Louis C. Tiffany's father. My father [Arthur J. Nash] *had* paid off almost all the bonds when C. L. Tiffany died. The remaining bonds were left to Louis C. Tiffany and he exchanged them for stock making him, principal stock holder. . . . I may not be quite right but it is virtually true."

71. The three photographs of workers that accompany this section are from a series made by the company in Arthur Saunders' shop at Tiffany Furnaces in April 1910. The first photograph shows Saunders trimming the neck of an urn. The second shows Harry Britton bringing glass to be worked by Saunders into a handle. The third photo shows Dave McNichol *(left)* and John Page *(right)* transferring the urn for finishing. The identity of the workers is annotated directly on Nash's photos, and agrees with the names supplied by Arthur Saunders; see Revi, *American Art Nouveau Glass,* 23.

72. Nash originally supplied a reference here to see the pictures presently on p. 49.

73. Only the first sentence and the photographs are relevant to the nominal subject of this section—namely, the first glass made by Arthur Nash for Tiffany. The 6½-inch-high vase, based on the form of a rosewater sprinkler, was signed "L.C.T.—First Piece" but this was undoubtedly a later addition. The Nashes owned this piece before selling it to Neil Reisner; see Revi, *American Art Nouveau Glass*, 44. The photo on p. 51 of our book comes from p. 63 of the album with photographs of early glass. In that album Leslie Nash wrote the absolutely erroneous caption "Mad[e] about 1912" and then carried the error over to his manuscript. The photo on p. 49 of our book must also be from that same series of early photos, and similar groupings of similar vases can be found, but this exact photo is no longer in the album. This suggests that the album was partially dismembered; indeed, there is a major gap between pages 48 and 55.

74. Nash frequently returned to this theme in his text and in his marginal notations on drawings and photographs. He thought of himself as a masculine, sensible businessman, in opposition to Tiffany, whom he characterized as soft and unconcerned with the practicalities of fabrication and the profit motive. Indeed, this is just where Tiffany's genius lay, and, fortunately, he had the where-withal to support this corporate position.

75. It may well be that Nash developed one or more formulas for iridescent glass while he worked at the Webb factories. For example, Webb made a line of iridescent Bronze Glass that was being sold by Tiffany & Co. in the late 1870s. The question, though, is whether Nash's two vases were actually made in England. Although his claim was accepted by Revi (*American Art Nouveau Glass*, 30), the freely manipulated forms and the feathered decoration of these two vases are not readily associated with Webb's more traditional English wares. On the other hand, they correspond exactly with the glass made at Corona. The bottle, for example, is almost identical to one in the Smithsonian Institution (inv. no. 96.434), and to another bought in 1897 by the Cincinnati Art Museum (inv. no. 1897.125). It may well be that Leslie Nash was misled by the fact that the bottoms of the two pieces bore the marks "B1" and "B2," which corresponded to the English formulas. Always anxious to demonstrate his father's importance in the development of Favrile glass, Leslie may have jumped to the conclusion that the vases had been made in England.

76. Nash has again conflated the temporal sequence. When he arrived in 1908, the company was Tiffany Furnaces. The name and officers he cites refers to the period after January 6, 1920.

77. The coloristic effects described here were exploited in the late nineteenth century by American glasshouses to create lines of art glass such as Amberina and Peachblow.

78. Nash is referring to the Boston and Sandwich Glass Company, which was active while Arthur Nash was still in England, closing only in 1888.

79. "Cypriote glass" refers to the Ancient glass that was excavated on Cyprus by Louis P. di Cesnola. The type of iridescence and textured surface caused by its decomposition while buried inspired Tiffany and Arthur J. Nash well before Leslie Nash came on the scene.

"Cypriote" effects appear, for example, on one of the early vases in the Havemeyer collection (inv. no. 96.17.13) and on a vase purchased in 1900 by the Philadelphia Museum of Art (inv. no. 01-63).

80. Nash appended a note: "(This picture is a photograph copy of a page that appeared in a Supplement to The Bulletin Of The Metropolitan Museum Of Art in 1911, entitled 'The Room of Ancient Glass.')."

81. For examples of this tableware, see Paul Doros, *The Tiffany Collection of the Chrysler Museum at Norfolk* (Norfolk: 1978), 80–81, cat. nos. 122–23.

82. For publicity promoting its introduction, see Elizabeth Lounsbery, "Aquamarine Glass," *American Homes and Gardens* 10 (December 1913), 419, 441. In one of his early drafts of this section, Nash incorrectly claimed that aquamarine glass had been introduced in 1919.

83. This photograph of the aquamarine vase with waterlilies has several sets of annotations. One is Arthur J. Nash's script initials and "Proof No 2." Leslie Nash's annotations are "Gold Medal 1900" (which does not seem a probable date), "waterlily 16" tall/ solid glass $300.00"

84. This compilation is copied from a Tiffany brochure, *Tiffany Favrile Glass*. In fact, the draft Nash gave his secretary to type was the actual brochure page pasted down, with the penciled script, "There must be some merit . . ."

85. The text that follows seems to refer to the coded system that was used to store the chemicals and which, like the Nashes' coded formula books, was a way of guaranteeing the secrets of their glass-making. See the description of this coded storage system on pp. 58–59.

86. The recipient was actually John McE. Bowman, whose bachelor dinner was given in the Biltmore Hotel, New York, on June 20, 1919. Lucius Boomer was president of the Waldorf Astoria Corporation from 1916 to 1934. The cup is now in the Corning Museum; see p. 220.

87. This claim is slightly misleading. Tiffany had introduced electric lamps just prior to 1900. Leslie expanded the repertoire of designs in this area and, at the same time, probably curtailed the production of fuel lamps.

88. While the tulip shade and pottery base are standard Tiffany designs, the butterfly finial is not. It must be something Leslie Nash had either fabricated or added ad hoc.

89. This comment is of extreme interest. Whereas elsewhere Leslie Nash complained that Tiffany never had any ideas, here he reveals how Tiffany was often inspired to start new experiments and how he was especially stimulated by his annual trips to Europe.

90. Edwin Bok, editor of the *Ladies' Home Journal*, had been inspired to turn to Tiffany after the successful reception in New York of the mosaic intended for Mexico City. The design was commissioned from Maxfield Parrish in about 1914; when the completed *Dream Garden* was provisionally exhibited in New York, supposedly some seven thousand visitors came to view it. It was then shipped to Philadelphia and installed over a period of six months. It was unveiled in 1916 to great acclaim.

91. The completed mosaic was exhibited in New York in April 1911 before being shipped to Mexico City; see the firm's brochure issued at the time: *Mosaic Curtain for the National Theater of Mexico*. It was then installed in 1912. Nash's typescript shows that he first assigned the date 1932 and later changed it to 1922. The actual history of the commission proves to have been different from what Nash remembered, and more complicated than is generally believed. For a full account see Juan Urquiaza and Victor Jiménez, *La Construccion del Palacio de Bellas Artes* (Mexico City: 1984); we are especially indebted to Alejandra Escudero for her help in explaining the commission. Around 1907–08 preliminary plans for the interior of the theater were submitted by the Hungarian designer Géza Maroti, the Italian Giovanni Beltrami, and Tiffany Studios. The commission for the allegorical mosaic on the proscenium arch was awarded to Maroti and Aladar Körösföi, and was executed by the Budapest firm Róth Miksa. Likewise, the famous mosaic glass curtain showing the two volcanoes of Popocatepetl and Ixtacchuatl was to have been executed from a design by Maroti, but then the contract was awarded to Tiffany in November 1909. The widespread tradition that the curtain was designed by Dr. Atl (the pseudonym of Gerardo Murillo) proves incorrect. The curtain was executed from a landscape painted by Tiffany employee Harry Stoner.

    The illustration of the theater curtain that Nash used was only a postcard (though he had tried to get a photograph from Mexico), and on the reverse side of the card he wrote, "The great curtain my big glass job LHN."

92. Preceding this section of illustrations are two pages with Nash's extended aside to the hypothetical editor: "EDITOR/PLEASE NOTE FOLLOWING/REMARKS/The Clippings and Photos on the following pages, 144—145—146—148—149—150 and 152, have been taken from the Tiffany Studios Book 'Ecclesiastical Department Tiffany Studios' Copyrighted and printed 1913 & 1922. This material is NOT to be used as such, but I have included *it* here to show the importance of Favrile glass windows and Mosaics Executed by The Tiffany Studios. Note all Tiffany Studios windows and Mosaics were made of Favrile glass. Therefore it is my suggestion, if the cost will not be to excessive, that two or three color pictures of the following beautiful examples of Tiffany windows be placed in this part of book.

    "Russell Sage Memorial Window, First Presbyterian Church, Far Rockaway, L.I., N.Y.

    "'The Celestial Hierarchy' Window, Chancel of the church of St. Michael's And All Angels, New York City, N.Y.

    "'The Sower' Window, Dr. Herbert Scott's church, Connecticut Ave. & Bancroft Place, Washington, D.C. (This window is about the same size as the Russell Sage Window).

    "(This page for Editors referance, only)"

    Nash also intended to have another image, as is indicated by an inserted page with the following directions. "COLOR PLATE Suggest color picture of window at— Dr. Herbert Scott's Church, Connecticut Ave & Bancroft Place, Washington, D.C.—Name Of The Window 'The Sower'—Note—(I regret to say That I do not have any photo of this window)"

93. Subsequent to the typing of the poet's name, Nash found his clipping of the poem and realized that it had been mistranscribed. He thought the proper family name was "Schriggs," but it proves to be "Scruggs." The poem, originally published by Ogelthorpe University Press in 1933, is reprinted here with that university's kind permission.

94. The technique of laminating five layers of glass and etching them to provide the details of faces, hands, and feet was used for *The Bathers*, the window that Tiffany installed in Laurelton Hall and which he considered a high point of his career.

95. The designation *Samian* has not been preserved in modern usage. Thus it is significant that Joseph Briggs, the business manager of Tiffany Studios, used it in relation to vases (Tiffany registration numbers 5015E and 5015B) in his collection that were later donated to the Haworth Art Gallery (see p. 216). Modern scholars have wrongly thought that *Samian* referred to the shapes of the vases; see Rüdiger Joppien, ed., *Louis C. Tiffany, Meisterwerke des amerikanischen Jugendstils*, exh. cat. (Hamburg: Museum für Kunst und Gewerbe, 1999), 252, cat. nos. 175–76. In fact, the term comes from a type of Roman ceramic ware, also known as *terra sigillata*, which is covered with a shiny red oxidized slip containing illite.

96. At first Nash supplied the date "1909–1910," but then penned in "1911." In this instance, his first estimate may have been more correct because Samian Red vases were already on exhibit in early 1911, which means that they must have been in production before the end of the previous year—i.e., 1910. See "Interior Decoration," *American Art News* 9 (25 February 1911), 8: "The Tiffany studios are . . . showing in great variety of shapes, some beautiful examples of turquoise glass, a revival of the effects of Egyptian glazes and colorings of the Tel-el-Amarna period and some fine reproductions of Samian reds."

    One wonders if Samian Red was different from other reds, because Tiffany was already producing red glass vases by 1905; see "Around the Studios," *American Art News* 3 (4 March 1905), 5: "Recently a new and beautiful shade of red has been produced in the Favrile glass. . . ."

97. The famed fete, celebrating Tiffany's sixty-fifth birthday, took place on February 4, 1913, and featured elaborate stage sets and costumes, as well as dancing by Ruth St. Denis.

98. A number of these desk sets employ enamels but of a simpler, more commercial type than those which had been used at the turn of the century. They probably correspond to the reopening of the enamel department by Nash in 1919.

99. The basic concept—as displayed here—of creating a new object by adapting the design of an older object in The Metropolitan Museum of Art derives from the program instituted by the museum itself; see Christine W. Laidlaw, "The Metropolitan Museum of Art and Modern Design, 1913–1926," *Journal of Decorative and Propaganda Arts*, 8 (Spring 1988), 88–103.

100. A copy of a German price list is preserved in Leslie Nash's large scrapbook. These color photographs, printed in Germany, confirm the nature of this export business. Most of the pieces are small and undecorated, and even the decorated pieces are of simple commercial types.

101. The process is the traditional method of slip casting. Nash's idea that the designs were first worked out in metal is somewhat misleading. The molds for the first ceramics, made several years before his arrival, were created by recasting some of the already realized enameled copper vases.

102. Originally, Nash supplied her family name of "Helmus" but then discreetly crossed it out. It is legible in earlier drafts.

103. The dancer is identified as Martha Lorber in a manuscript version of this story in Nash's estate, and also in the list of stories he compiled on page 98 of the album with photographs of early glass.

104. Leslie Nash's sense of chronology is off. Arthur Nash died on March 13, 1934, at the age of 84 years, 4 months, and 13 days, according to the official burial record.

105. This page was found among the loose, previously typed drafts of Leslie Nash's text still with the Nash family. According to a note written across the top by John Nash on March 11, 1958, the page was removed from the book at the request of Betty Nash, Leslie's widow. Although she wished to suppress it, we believe it brings the manuscript to a more definitive conclusion. Moreover, its tale of Anglophobia is as illuminating as it is shocking.

106. On page 99 of his album with photographs of early glass, Leslie noted the names of the members of the Nash family who arrived in the United States in 1892: "and Norman, who died that same year."

107. Added on a last page is an interesting "Appendix" written by Leslie's son, John W. Nash: "A Note To The Editor.—It was my father's suggestion that an Appendix could be added to this book in order to provide the Collectors with a partial check list of Tiffany 'Favrile' Glass.

"In looking over our material, I find that I could provide about forty or fifty stockroom photographs, showing approximately 400 pieces of 'Favrile' glass. This would be a photographic check list. Discriptions of size, color, and list price, cannot be included. However, the value of a check list of shapes would be immeasurable. An example of the type of stockroom photo that I am referring to can be seen on pages 37 and 37-A, of this book [John Nash was referring to the album with more than sixty photographs of early Favrile glass].

"My father suggested that I not make these Copy negatives until he had discussed the matter with the Editors, and until such time as the publishers had committed themselves to publishing the book. The extra time and expense being rather high for a speculative venture.

"My father did not wish this book to be a catalogue of sizes and shapes, however, I think he realized the value of an appendix in helping to increase the desireability of the book, thereby extending the potential market of sales.

"Should this book be acceptable in all other ways, I shall be happy to discuss the Appendix in further detail.—JOHN W. NASH"

108. See Martin Eidelberg, "Tiffany's Early Glass Vessels," Antiques 137 (February 1990), 502–15; Rüdiger Joppien, "Kunstgläser," in Joppien, ed., Louis C. Tiffany, Meisterwerke des amerikanischen Jugendstils, 96–185.

109. A 1926 letter from Arthur J. Nash claimed that it came from an old Saxon word meaning "handwrought"; reproduced in Hugh F. McKean, The Treasures of Tiffany (Chicago: 1982), 43.

110. The Art Work of Louis C. Tiffany, 25. There was yet another change to come: by the spring of 1894, the monogram of the Tiffany Glass and Decorating Company began to be associated with the glass and was used on round paper labels.

111. See pages 29, 34, 36, 39, and 42 of Nash's album of photographs of early glass.

112. See pages 27, 28, 36, 38, and 44 of Nash's album of photographs; also see those illustrated in Nash's Tiffany Favrile Glass (pp. 48, 53), and in his scrapbook (p. 224).

113. See footnote 73. As will be seen, he also removed at least one photograph from one of the albums of pottery photographs for use in his manuscript Tiffany Favrile Glass.

114. See pages 36, 39, 58, 63, 70, 72 of Nash's album of photographs of early glass.

115. See Martin Eidelberg, "Tiffany Favrile Pottery," Connoisseur 169 (September 1968), 55–61.

116. For a report of his experimentation, see Keramic Studio 2 (December 1900), 161.

117. There is no reference to them in the Tiffany & Co. Blue Book for 1905 (dated October 31, 1904), but they are listed in the 1906 Blue Book (dated October 31, 1905), 459, 527.

118. See, respectively, A. V. Rose, "The Thirteenth Annual Exhibition of the New York Society of Keramic Arts," American Pottery Gazette 1 (May 1905), 24, and L'Art décoratif aux salons de 1906 (ed. Guerinet), pl. 143–44.

119. See the Tiffany Furnaces advertisement in International Studio 38 (November 1908). A number of printed images of these lamps from an unidentified source were pasted into Nash's large scrapbook.

120. The pottery was listed in Tiffany & Co.'s Blue Book of 1917, p. 442, but was not listed in the 1919 edition.

121. See Clara Ruge, "Amerikanische Keramik," Dekorative Kunst 14 (January 1906), 175. Ruge, a German critic living in New York, often reported on American developments.

122. See Clara Ruge, "American Ceramics—A Brief Review of Progress," International Studio 28 (March 1906), xxiii. One illustration is of the vase with floral decoration at the top left of our p. 177, and the other is of the vase with a green textured glaze at the top right of our p. 184.

123. Other sets of company photographs have related sets of numbers. For example, in the Nash archives is a series of photographs of the workers in the glass and metal department, some of which are numbered continuously from 13601 to 13605. However, there is no system of suffix numbers; rather, each number is simply sequential. Another set of these views was in the collection of the glassblower Jimmy Stewart; see Koch, Louis C. Tiffany's Glass—Bronzes—Lamps, 27, 51, 52, 85. The first of Stewart's photographs is

numbered, and its number agrees with the counterpart in Nash's set. A third set of these photographs was in the collection of Arthur Saunders, but it is unnumbered; see Revi, *American Art Nouveau Glass*, 23, 24, 28. According to Saunders, the photographs were taken in April 1910.

124. Inv. No. 14236; donated by Louis C. Tiffany, June 28, 1907. The vase has an engraved signature, "L. C. Tiffany/ Salon 1906/ 2023 C." See Joppien, *Louis C. Tiffany, Meisterwerke des amerikanischen Jugendstils,* 252, cat. no. 168.

125. A second extant example is in the Morse Museum, Winter Park, Florida; see Alice Cooney Frelinghuysen, *American Art Pottery, Selections from the Charles Hosmer Morse Museum of American Art*, exh. cat. (Orlando: Museum of Art, 1995), 125. A third is in a private collection.

BIBLIOGRAPHY

Amaya, Mario. *Tiffany Glass* (New York and London: 1967).

Bing, Samuel [sic]. *Artistic America, Tiffany Glass, and Art Nouveau*, ed. Robert Koch (Cambridge, Massachusetts: 1970).

De Kay, Charles. *The Art Work of Louis C. Tiffany* (Garden City, New York: 1914).

Doros, Paul E. *The Tiffany Collection of the Chrysler Museum at Norfolk* (Norfolk, Virginia: Chrysler Museum, 1978).

Duncan, Alastair. *Louis Comfort Tiffany* (New York: 1992).

———. *Tiffany at Auction* (New York: 1981).

———. *Tiffany Windows* (New York: 1980).

———, Martin Eidelberg, and Neil Harris. *Masterworks of Louis Comfort Tiffany* (New York and London: 1989).

———, and Tsuneo Yoshimizu. *Masterworks of Louis Comfort Tiffany* (Tokyo: Tokyo Metropolitan Teien Art Museum, 1991).

Eidelberg, Martin. "Tiffany Favrile Pottery," *Connoisseur* 169 (September 1968), 55–6l.

———. "Tiffany's Early Glass Vessels," *Antiques* 137 (February 1990), 502–15.

Feld, Stuart P. " 'Nature in Her Most Seductive Aspects': Louis Comfort Tiffany's Favrile Glass," *The Metropolitan Museum of Art Bulletin* 21 (November 1962), 101–12.

Frelinghuysen, Alice Cooney. "Louis Comfort Tiffany at The Metropolitan Museum," *The Metropolitan Museum of Art Bulletin* 56 (Summer 1998), 3–100.

Horiuchi, Takeo, ed. *The World of Louis Comfort Tiffany: A Selection from the Anchorman Collection* (Matsue: 1994).

Joppien, Rüdiger, ed. *Louis C. Tiffany, Meisterwerke des amerikanischen Jugendstils*, exh. cat. (Hamburg: Museum für Kunst und Gewerbe, 1999).

Koch, Robert. *Louis Comfort Tiffany 1848–1933*, exh. cat. (New York: Museum of Contemporary Crafts of the American Craftsmen's Council, 1958).

———. *Louis C. Tiffany, Rebel in Glass* (New York: 1964).

———. *Louis C. Tiffany's Glass—Bronzes—Lamps* (New York: 1971).

Loring, John. *Tiffany's 150 Years* (Garden City: 1987).

Mayer, Roberta A., and Caroline K. Lane. "Disassociating the 'Associated Artists': The Early Business Ventures of Louis C. Tiffany, Candace T. Wheeler, and Lockwood de Forest," *Studies in the Decorative Arts* 8 (Spring/Summer 2001), 2–36.

McKean, Hugh. *The "Lost" Treasures of Louis Comfort Tiffany* (New York: 1980).

———. *The Treasures of Tiffany* (Chicago: 1982).

Neustadt, Egon. *The Lamps of Tiffany* (New York: 1970).

Revi, Albert Christian. *American Art Nouveau Glass* (Exton, Pennsylvania: 1968).

Speenburgh, Gertrude. *The Arts of the Tiffanys* (Chicago: 1956).

Zapata, Janet. *The Jewelry and Enamels of Louis Comfort Tiffany* (New York: 1993).

INDEX

235